MALI
in Pictures

Francesca Davis Di Piazza

Twenty-First Century Books

Contents

Twenty-First Century Books
A division of Lerner Publishing Group
241 First Avenue North
Minneapolis, MN 55401 U.S.A.

Website address: www.lernerbooks.com

web enhanced @ www.vgsbooks.com

CULTURAL LIFE 48

► Religion. The Arts. Literature and
Communications. Music. Sports, Recreation, and
Holidays. Food.

THE ECONOMY 58

► Agriculture and Fishing. Industry, Manufacturing,
and Mining. Services, Transportation, and Energy.
The Future.

FOR MORE INFORMATION

Library of Congress Cataloging-in-Publication Data

Di Piazza, Francesca Davis.
    Mali in pictures / by Francesca Davis DiPiazza.—Rev. & expanded.
        p.   cm. — (Visual geography series)
    Includes bibliographical references and index.
    ISBN-13: 978-0-8225-6591-8 (lib. bdg. : alk. paper)
    ISBN-10: 0-8225-6591-9 (lib. bdg. : alk. paper)
    1. Mali—Juvenile literature. 2. Mali—Pictorial works—Juvenile literature. I. Title. II. Visual geography
series (Minneapolis, Minn.)
DT551.22.D57 2007
 966.23—dc22   2006005615

Manufactured in the United States of America
1 2 3 4 5 6 - BP - 12 11 10 09 08 07

INTRODUCTION

People sometimes use the phrase, "From here to Tombouctou (or Timbuktu)," meaning that someplace is mysterious and very far away. But many people don't know where Tombouctou actually is. It is a fabled trading city on the Niger River in the landlocked West African nation of Mali.

Europeans did not reach Tombouctou until the nineteenth century. To reach the city from places along the Mediterranean Sea to the north, a traveler had to cross more than 1,000 miles (1,609 km) of the burning, waterless Sahara. To approach from the south, from the Atlantic Ocean, a traveler faced close to 600 miles (966 km) of thick forest full of dangerous animals. Crocodiles and lions attack some people, but the deadliest tropical animals are tiny ones. Malaria-carrying mosquitoes are more dangerous than any mammal.

Mali is a country of 13.4 million people. The nation lies on the southern edge of the Sahara, the world's largest desert. People herd livestock in Mali's dry northern and central regions. The Niger River,

Africa's third-largest river, is Mali's lifeline in the south. Landlocked with no coastlines, Mali relies on the river for water, fish, trade, and transportation. Most of Mali's people live in the southern fertile grasslands. They are mainly farmers, fishers, and traders.

Mali was once the home of the great empires of Ghana, Mali, and Songhai. For centuries, these rich empires traded gold and slaves for salt and textiles from North African markets along the Mediterranean Sea. Caravans (traveling groups) of camels and merchants relied on desert guides to make the long trip across the Sahara.

In the eleventh century, Islamic armies from North Africa conquered Mali. Gradually, most of the area's people accepted the Islamic religion. Tombouctou—located where the Niger River meets the Sahara—became a great trade city. It also became an international center for Islamic studies, reaching a high level of civilization.

Between the sixteenth and the nineteenth centuries, slave raiders supplied West African people to the European slave trade.

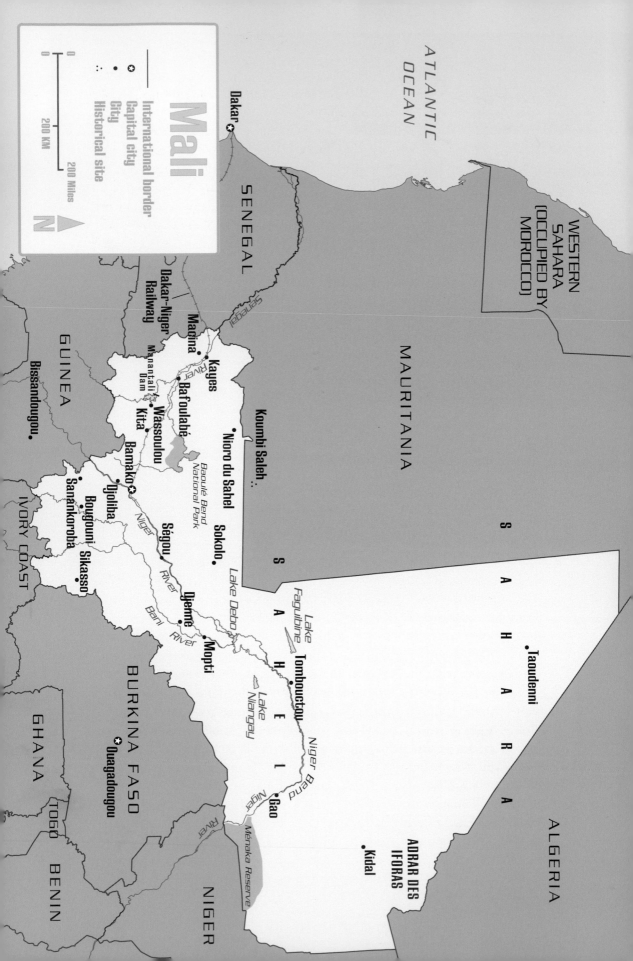

During this time, trade patterns shifted, and Mali and Tombouctou's greatness faded.

By the 1800s, some Africans wanted to spread Islam throughout West Africa. They also hoped to prevent Europeans—particularly the French—from taking over. With these goals in mind, African leaders established several small states, which included much of Mali's land. By the late 1890s, however, French troops had subdued the forces of the Islamic realms. France made the territory part of its vast African colonial empire. Mali was known as French Sudan under colonial rule.

Mali achieved independence in 1960, along with other French territories in West Africa. In 1968 Moussa Traoré led a government takeover and took power. Beginning in the 1970s, severe droughts turned large portions of Mali into desert. Unpredictable rainfall hurt traditional living patterns and livelihoods. Many of the nation's herders—such as the Fulbé and the Tuareg, who live in central and northern Mali—lost much of their livestock. As a result of poor harvests, many Malians suffered from malnutrition or died.

Prodemocracy groups demonstrated against Traoré's corrupt rule. But Traoré ruled Mali as a dictator until 1991, when a coup (government overthrow) against him led to the election of Alpha Oumar Konare. After two terms of political and economic improvements, Konare stepped down in 2002. In a peaceful, democratic election, Amadou Toumani Touré emerged the winner. He was the man who had overthrown the regime of Traoré eleven years earlier. The goals of Touré's government include encouraging trade, developing industry and roads, and improving educational and health systems.

Mali remains one of the world's poorest nations. It struggles with few resources, low export income, drought, and ongoing food shortages. According to the United Nations Human Development Index (HDI), Mali ranks 172 out of 175 countries. The HDI measures a number of key indicators of social well-being. Mali's measurements reflect the nation's lack of health care, education, and other social services.

In spite of their struggles, Malians are famous for having one of the most vibrant cultures in Africa. One of Mali's most popular exports is its dynamic music. Its masks and sculptures are found in art museums all over the world. In recent years, the nation has drawn admiration for its peaceful transition from dictatorship to a stable democracy. Mali, largely a Muslim country, has also joined the United States and other nations in the global war on terrorism. In the twenty-first century, Mali's political stability offers hope that Mali will be able to gain self-sufficiency.

THE LAND

Mali is the largest country in West Africa. The nation covers 478,842 square miles (1,240,192 sq. km)—about the size of Texas and California combined. Moving clockwise from the northeast, Mali's seven neighbors are Algeria, Niger, Burkina Faso, Ivory Coast (Côte d'Ivoire), Guinea, Senegal, and Mauritania. Mali is surrounded by land and has no access to the ocean. Senegal's Atlantic Ocean coast lies about 600 miles (966 km) west of Mali's capital, Bamako. Ivory Coast's Atlantic shore lies about 500 miles (804 km) south of Bamako.

◉ Topography

Mali's generally flat territory consists of three main regions. The Sahara (Arabic for "desert") covers the northern half of the country. The Sahel (Arabic for "shore"), a semidesert zone, forms a band across the center of the country. Fertile savanna (grassland) is found in southern Mali.

Mali's northern region is part of the Sahara. The desert extends across North Africa for 3.5 million square miles (9 million sq. km), about the size of the United States. Most of the desert is made up of flat, rocky plains that almost never receive rain. In some places, a region of shifting sand dunes, called an *erg*, appears. A mountainous region, Adrar des Iforas, rises in northeastern Mali. Tuareg people and other desert nomads live in the Sahara. They move with their herds of animals to find pasture and water at oases (places where water comes near the desert's surface). Even in modern times, camels often make the most reliable form of transportation in the desert.

The Sahel is a band of semidesert along the southern edge of the Sahara. The Sahel forms Mali's central region. Herders raise live-stock here. Rainfall is unreliable, and drought in recent years has hit the region hard. In 2004 swarms of locusts (grasshopper-like flying insects) devastated crops and grazing lands. Many thousands of animals died. Continuing poor harvests threaten more than

The desert-dwelling Tuareg nomads can find their way in the Sahara without maps or roads. They read many different signs, such as the ripples of a sand dune, bird flight, and the stars at night. An ancient Tuareg saying advises, "If you get lost, remain calm for the desert is calm."

one million people in the Sahel with starvation.

South of the Sahel is a vast inland delta, or fertile flood land. Most Malians live in this Niger Delta region formed by the Niger River and its main tributary (feeder river), the Bani. The area contains some of the richest farmland in Africa. Farmers raise crops and animals in the region's grasslands. Fishers make their living from the rivers and lakes. The rivers have many branches and form swamps and lakes. Some dry up in the dry season, but two bodies of water —Lake Debo and Lake Faguibine—retain water all year-round. Disease-carrying mosquitoes breed in warm, wet areas, and malaria is a health hazard in the south.

Although most of Mali is flat, several elevated features appear in the south. The Bandiagara Ridge is a series of cliffs that runs for about 150 miles (241 km) from southwest to northeast. These cliffs are part of the Dogon Plateau. The Dogon people, one of Mali's ethnic groups, build their houses into the cliffs. The Hombori Mountains, another major landform, are made of sandstone. The tallest mountain in the

The cliff dwellings of the Dogon people are made primarily of mud and rock, supported by wood frames. Recently, the Dogon have begun to abandon their cliff dwellings in favor of villages at the foot of the Dogon Plateau.

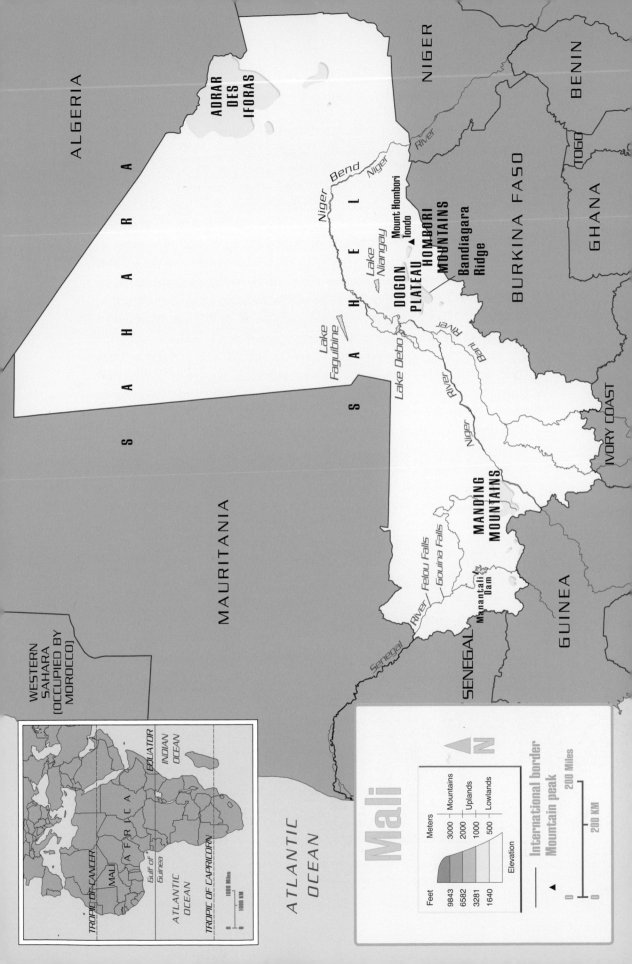

range and in the country, Mount Hombori Tondo, rises to 3,789 feet (1,155 meters). The Manding Mountains stretch from the nation's western border almost to the capital city of Bamako. These highlands climb to 1,500 feet (457 m) above sea level.

Rivers

Two large rivers—the Niger and the Senegal—provide Mali with water. The Niger is the third-longest waterway in Africa, after the Nile and Congo rivers. It begins its 2,600-mile (4,183 km) course in Guinea. Flowing northeastward, the Niger enters Mali near Bamako. A network of the river's branches creates the country's central delta region. On the edge of the Sahara, near Tombouctou, the Niger changes direction. It begins to flow in a southeastern direction, forming a curve called the Niger Bend. Boats carry fishers, passengers, and goods on the river. The Bani, the Niger's main tributary in Mali, joins the Niger at Mopti. It is also an important route for goods and people. Outside of Mali, rapids and waterfalls on the Niger prevent boats from traveling all the way to the ocean. In Nigeria the Niger River empties into the Gulf of Guinea, an arm of the Atlantic Ocean.

The Senegal River rises in Guinea and flows northwestward for 560 miles (901 km). In Mali the Gouina Falls and the Felou Falls break the course of the Senegal. In April, at the end of the dry season,

The Niger River is an important transportation route, traveled by large passenger ferries and smaller pirogues (canoes).

the river is reduced to a shallow stream. The Senegal's branches irrigate the land between the southwestern towns of Kayes and Kita. The river cuts through Senegal and Mauritania before emptying into the Atlantic Ocean.

Climate

Mali's temperatures stay fairly high year-round. Malians use the country's annual cycle of rainfall to mark the seasons. The climate varies from region to region, but overall the weather is wettest from June to September. Winds affect rainfall and temperature levels. Extremely dry, hot winds called harmattans form in the Sahara. They bring clouds of dust that make it hard to see and that cover everything with grit as they blow southward. Winds from the Gulf of Guinea carry moisture and slightly lower temperatures to southern Mali.

Less than 10 inches (25 centimeters) of rain fall in the Sahara every year. Some areas may go for years with no rain. Mali's desert often reaches temperatures of 120°F (49°C) during the day. There are no clouds to trap the desert heat once the sun sets. Therefore, the Sahara's temperature plunges every night, falling as low as 40°F (4°C).

In the Sahel, rainfall varies from 7 to 20 inches (18 to 51 cm) a year. Temperatures generally stay between 80°F (27°C) and 100°F (38°C). Occasional drought is a natural feature of the Sahel. But serious shortages of rain beginning in the 1970s threaten and kill increasing numbers of animals, plants, and people.

The far south of Mali receives about 60 inches (152 cm) of rainfall annually. Temperatures range between 75°F (24°C) and 95°F (35°C) throughout southern Mali. High humidity (moisture levels in the air) makes the air feel heavy and sticky.

Flora and Fauna

Mali has three areas of vegetation that match the country's three

TROPIC OF CANCER

On world maps, the Tropic of Cancer is an imaginary line that runs through many lands, including northern Mali. The line is the northern border of the tropics— the regions around the equator (midway between the North and South Poles). Temperatures in the tropics stay about the same year-round. The Tropic of Cancer marks the northernmost point where the sun can appear directly overhead. Once a year, at noon on the summer solstice (June 20, 21, or 22), the sun shines directly down on the Tropic of Cancer.

MALI'S DESERT ELEPHANTS

Elephants once roamed all over West Africa, but poachers killed most of them for their valuable ivory tusks. Only a few herds remain, including one of about four hundred animals in Mali's Sahel region. These elephants travel about 35 miles (56 km) a day, migrating from waterhole to waterhole. They travel at night and rest under acacia trees in the daytime, when the temperature climbs to 120°F (49°C). Local people traditionally left the elephants alone, but years of drought have changed that. As the supply of wild plants dwindle, the elephants have begun to eat people's crops. Farmers protect their fields with guns. Scientists working with Mali's nature conservation department have attached tracking collars to some of the elephants. They are studying the elephants' travels. They hope to protect both the animals and the people's food and water.

regions. Only a few kinds of hardy, thorny plants can survive the harsh conditions of the Sahara.

The Sahel zone is sparsely vegetated with tough plants that can live for long periods without rain. The tiny, spiky burrs of cram-cram grasses scatter across the land, sticking to anything that moves. Thorny acacia trees and doum palms grow in the dry soil. The baobab tree holds water in its barkless trunk. This squat tree is often as wide as it is tall (about 50 feet, or 15 meters). Its twisting branches look like wild hair. *Baobab* comes from Arabic *bu hibab*, meaning "fruit with many seeds." The tree's sour fruit can be eaten.

Mali's wooded grasslands begin south of Bamako. Some forests are located along the region's rivers. The most common trees are silk-cotton trees and shea trees. People harvest shea tree seeds for their edible fat called shea butter. Malians also plant many mango fruit trees in the area. The French first brought mango trees from Asia. Mali's farmland is in the south, where small plots yield cereal grains, root crops, and cotton.

For centuries, Malian farmers have cleared the land to grow food or to create pastureland for cattle, sheep, and goats. Because human activity destroys natural habitats, few large wild animals remain in the country. A limited number of lions and giraffes live in Mali. A few hundred desert elephants struggle for survival in the Sahel. Several different kinds of antelope make their homes in scattered areas of the country. Wild pigs live in forested areas, and warthogs are found on the savanna. Hyenas, jackals, and small wild cats are common. Baboons and several kinds of monkeys inhabit national parks. Chimpanzees remain in the extreme south.

About two hundred kinds of fish swim in Mali's rivers, lakes, and ponds. Fishers catch carp, catfish, perch, Nile perch, and other freshwater species. Hippopotamuses dwell along the Niger and the Bani. Rivers are also home to otters, turtles, and manatees, or sea cows.

Reptiles are widespread in Mali. Lizards thrive in all the nation's climates. Snakes are common, varying from the harmless 15 foot (5 m) python to the poisonous 3 foot (1 m) puff adder. Crocodiles dwell along rivers, although they have become less common. Malians traditionally consider crocodiles sacred.

Despite their friendly looks, hippos are responsible for more human deaths than any other mammal in Africa. They are very territorial and will charge people who come too close, trampling them or biting them with their large tusked mouths.

Many species of birds, including an occasional ostrich, thrive in the inland delta and the Niger Bend. Rollers and bee-eaters display brilliant blue, scarlet, and gold feathers. These birds eat flying insects, including bees. The Mali firefinch is the only species that is endemic, or unique, to Mali. This small red bird lives all over the country.

Mali is rich in insect life. Termites build mounds up to 9 feet (3 m) tall. The mounds are made of individual grains of sand or dirt glued together with the termite's sticky saliva. Scorpions stay cool under rocks in Mali's hot, dry lands. The most dangerous animal in the delta is the female *Anopheles* mosquito, which carries malaria.

Some licensed hunting and a lot of poaching (illegal killing) occur in Mali's two national parks—Baoulé Bend National Park in the west and Ménaka Reserve in the east. Giraffes, elephants, antelope, lions, and hippos inhabit these semiprotected areas.

Natural Resources and Environmental Concerns

The Niger River is Mali's most important natural resource. It brings water to a land with little rain and no coastline. The river provides fish and transportation routes. Its enormous fertile delta allows farmers to raise grains and herd livestock.

Mali has few mineral resources. Gold and salt are the main minerals that Mali exploits. Miners also produce limestone and phosphate (an key ingredient in fertilizer).

Mali holds the potential to attract tourists. Dramatic Saharan landscapes, boat trips on the Niger River, and sites of ancient empires all are important resources. Mali's many ethnic groups live together peacefully in the south, and the country is a friendly place to visit.

Mali faces major environmental challenges. The most urgent issue is desertification, or the process of dry lands turning to barren desert. Desertification results from natural stresses, such as drought, and from the heavy use of dry lands. Too many people struggling for essentials such as water, food, shelter, and fuel overstress the land.

Deforestation, or the loss of woodlands, is another serious concern for Mali. Wood supplies 90 percent of Mali's energy. People cut trees for cooking fuel and building

A street sign in French warns Malians that "brush fires cause desertification."

materials. The loss of trees contributes to desertification. Without tree roots to hold the soil in place, it dries up and blows away, leaving dry, barren land.

Natural disasters that strike Mali include drought, occasional Niger River floods, and locust swarms that strip crops bare. Locusts also eat the grasses animals depend on.

Mali once had bounteous wildlife. But due to many environmental factors, including overpopulation and poaching, most of Mali's large animal species have died out. Nineteen more animal species and six plant species in Mali may die out completely. The government of Mali works to address its environmental challenges. But poverty is the root of the problem. As long as people are desperate for food, fuel, and water, conservation efforts will be of secondary concern.

▷ Cities

Only about 30 percent of Mali's 13.4 million people live in cities. Throughout the country, many villages have fewer than 2,000 people. Most of these settlements lie near rivers or in areas where rainfall is plentiful.

BAMAKO, Mali's capital and largest city, has about 1 million people. Most of them earn at least part of their living from herding, fishing, or farming. In 1908 Bamako became the capital of the French

Bamako's Marché Rose market bustles with people buying and selling goods, from textiles and wood carvings to spices and medicines.

colony called French Sudan. When Mali gained independence in 1960, Bamako was a quiet, shady place on the western bank of the Niger River. Over time, the city expanded to the eastern bank. The commercial and administrative center of the nation, modern Bamako has a lively market area. The main area of the city also contains the Grand Mosque (an Islamic place of prayer), lavish homes, and government offices. Modern, cement houses with running water and electricity are scattered throughout the city. But most Malians in Bamako live in mud-brick dwellings. Some neighborhoods consist of run-down shacks, where people struggle to survive because they have no jobs.

SÉGOU (population 200,000), located along the Niger River, is Mali's second-largest city. Once the capital of a nineteenth-century African realm, the city also contains many colonial-era buildings from its days

as a French outpost. The Bambara—Mali's major ethnic group—are the main vendors in Ségou's market. They sell handmade masks, pottery, food, and other items.

SIKASSO (population 120,000) lies in the far southeastern part of the country, near Ivory Coast. Located in a well-watered area, the city contains much of Mali's Senufo population. Historically, the Senufo resisted being absorbed by other powers—both European and African. Their distinct culture survives in villages surrounding Sikasso.

MOPTI (population 90,000) is situated on several small connected islands where the Bani and the Niger rivers join. It is an important Islamic center and a thriving marketplace. Traders sell fish, salt, goats, firewood, pottery, and more at the busy port. Boat makers make pirogues (dugout wooden canoes), and tourists take rides on the river. The city is home to a mixture of Mali's many ethnic groups.

KAYES (population 65,000) lies in western Mali along the Senegal River near the Senegal border. The Dakar-Niger Railway connects Dakar, the capital of Senegal, to Kayes. Kayes also has a vital role as a river port city. In the rainy season, boats can travel westward from Kayes to the Atlantic Ocean.

Workers unload pirogues in **Mopti's busy port.**

 **The Djenné Mosque** is the largest mud-brick building in the world. The wooden poles that stick out from the mosque's walls are part of the frame that supports the bricks. Villagers also use the poles as ladders when the mosque must be repaired following the annual rainy season.

Historic Cities

As the center of several important African realms in ancient times, Mali contains evidence of highly developed civilizations. Some of these findings exist in the ruins of former cities, trade stations, and Islamic centers. Other ancient towns—such as Gao, Tombouctou, and Djenné—still survive.

Located on the Niger River in north central Mali, Gao (population 65,000) was once the capital of the Songhai Empire. This domain flourished in the fifteenth and sixteenth centuries. City planners rebuilt much of Gao in the twentieth century, and it is a thriving river port. Most buildings, however, are poorly constructed and crowded.

Founded in about 1100, Tombouctou (population 38,000) is located near the Niger River in central Mali. Its name means "well of Buktu" (a woman's name). A trade hub and center of Islamic learning and culture, the city flourished between 1200 and 1591. After Moroccan raiders from the north sacked Tombouctou in 1591, the city declined. Shifting sands weakened the earthen buildings, and most have crumbled. Several mosques remain standing, however. In modern times, little trade occurs. A yearly camel caravan still brings salt from northern mines.

 Visit www.vgsbooks.com for links to websites with additional information about the many things to see and do in Mali's cities, as well as links to websites about Mali's weather, natural resources, plants and animals, and more.

Archaeologists believe that Djenné (pronounced jeh-NAY), in south central Mali, is one of the oldest settlements in West Africa. In about 250 B.C., it was a settlement of round mud dwellings. By A.D. 800, the city had become an important trans-Saharan trading center. Djenné reached its height as a marketplace and Islamic center between the 1300s and the 1500s. It was declared a World Heritage Site in 1988. Modern Djenné has only 10,000 residents. Djenné's famous mud mosque draws visitors to the region. An excellent example of the local architectural style, the building requires yearly repairs after annual rains soften its outside walls.

HISTORY AND GOVERNMENT

Roughly ten thousand years ago, the southern Sahara had a wet climate. Heavy rainfall in the region of present-day Mali created a lush land that supported many wild animals. Families of Stone Age fishers and hunters moved to live near the land's bodies of water.

About 4000 B.C., however, the rainfall began to decrease. The region became drier and hotter. As the lakes dried up, the local people learned to gather root crops and to raise livestock. Eventually, the dry weather reduced food supplies and forced many populations south. They moved away from the expanding desert into the inland delta of the Niger.

Villages developed on the west central borders of Mali. The new residents cleared forests to plant grain. They grazed livestock on the grasslands. Climate changes, as well as the removal of local vegetation, helped the desert to spread even farther. By the 400s B.C., the Sahara was well established.

The desert might have cut off contact between the Mediterranean coast and the south if not for the introduction of camels. Middle

Eastern traders brought these animals to the Sahara in about A.D. 100. Because they can survive long periods without water, camels became the main form of desert transportation.

Over the next two hundred years, populations grew large enough in some parts of Mali to support trading centers. Loosely organized kingdoms emerged. Most of these kingdoms were made up of villages with local leaders. These kingdoms and the empires that followed them were patriarchal societies. That is, men had more political, economic, and social power than women.

The Ghana Empire

A federation of kingdoms called the Ghana Empire evolved about 300. (This empire is not related to the modern-day nation of Ghana.) *Ghana* means "king." The empire developed from farming settlements in western Mali and southeastern Mauritania. It had its capital at Kumbi Saleh (in Mauritania) and reached its peak between 700 and 1075. This strong empire earned its wealth from the control of Saharan trade routes. These were the only known paths through the Sahara. Merchants journeyed from the capital and other towns to North Africa's Mediterranean coast. Camel caravans from North Africa crossed the Sahara, carrying cloth, salt, and other products to southern regions. The Berbers controlled the northern sections of the Saharan traffic. The traders returned to North Africa with gold, leather goods, and human beings sold into slavery. (Slavery was an accepted institution in many ancient societies around the world.) Ghana also developed roads that went south to the Gulf of Guinea.

Members of the Soninke people ruled the empire. They made nearby ethnic groups subjects of their realm. Emperors charged taxes on goods that traveled along their commercial routes. The resulting income allowed the empire to keep a large army. This strong military force ensured the realm's continued control over trade.

Many of the merchants with whom the Soninke traders came in contact were Arabs from areas north and east of the empire. The Soninke's traditional African religion honored many spiritual forces. The Arabs had accepted a new, one-god religion called Islam in the seventh century. Traders brought the faith from the Arabian Peninsula to North Africa. Within one hundred years, the Berbers had accepted Islam.

In 1076 the Almoravids—an Islamic Berber dynasty (family of rulers)—sent troops to destroy the Ghana Empire and to take over its trade routes. Almoravid forces seized Kumbi Saleh. They made the realm an Islamic state. Although Soninke warriors recaptured the city about fifteen years later, the Ghana Empire continued to decline. During this period, people from Sosso—a kingdom ruled by Ghana— revolted. By 1203 Sosso troops had gained control of the capital.

⊙ The Mali Empire

The Mali Empire developed in the 1200s from a small Malinke kingdom located near the present-day boundary between Mali and Guinea. The Malinke kingdom was under Ghana's and later under Sosso's authority. But the Malinke wanted self-rule. A Malinke warrior-prince named Sundiata Keita led a successful war of independence against the Sosso kingdom in about 1230. *Sundiata* means "lion prince." He combined many other small Malinke units to form the Mali Empire. The realm was centered in present-day Guinea. Like the Ghana Empire, the Mali Empire became rich and powerful through Saharan trade.

In Malinke and other Malian societies, a special class of people called griots, or *djeliw*, were professional historians. Griots passed down history by word of mouth, usually through songs accompanied by traditional musical instruments. Modern historians use surviving ancient accounts to understand Mali's history. The most famous is the tale of the great leader Sundiata.

At its height in the thirteenth and fourteenth centuries, the empire included parts of present-day Mali, Senegal, Gambia, Guinea, Mauritania, Burkina Faso, and Niger. Although the majority of Mali's subjects held traditional African beliefs, the ruler and government officials were Muslims (followers of Islam).

Under the Malinke *mansa* (king) Musa, who reigned between 1312 and about 1337, Mali became well known to the Islamic world. In 1324 the ruler made the hajj—a pilgrimage (religious visit) to the holy Islamic city of Mecca, Saudi Arabia. The king traveled across the Sahara—a long, hard journey. His willingness to be absent from the realm showed his strong hold on the Mali throne.

Hundreds of people accompanied Mansa Musa. He increased his importance by distributing large amounts of gold to people along the route to Mecca. The trip made strong impressions on people. As a result, trans-Saharan trade increased dramatically, and Islamic scholars came to Mali. Soon after Mansa Musa's return, he gained control of the trade city of Gao in central Mali. In addition, the ruler established Tombouctou as an Islamic center of learning and trade.

The vast Mali Empire required skilled leaders. But after Mansa Musa died, few of his successors had the abilities to keep the realm together. Gradually, outlying areas came under the authority of other groups, including the Tuareg and the Songhai.

The Songhai Empire

Long established as a minor realm, the Songhai Empire increased in size and strength beginning in the mid-1300s. It soon began to absorb more territory, chiefly by taking over the Saharan trade routes that the Mali Empire once held.

THE NEED FOR SALT

For centuries, caravans of thousands of camels carried items southward through the Sahara to trade at the Niger River. Metal weapons, fine cloth, and jewelry were prized goods. But the main form of exchange was northern salt—extracted from seawater or mined in the desert—for central African gold. Salt was so valuable it was sometimes traded in equal weight for gold. In the 1400s, an Italian traveler, Alvise da Cada Mosto, wrote explaining the Malian need for salt: "At the season of the year of the great heats, their blood . . . putrefies [breaks up]. And if it were not for salt they would die." (Larry Brook, *Daily Life in Ancient and Modern Timbuktu*, [Minneapolis: Runestone, 1999], 19.) Modern scientists agree. Human blood contains salt, and our bodies must have salt for good health.

The Songhai emperor Sonni Ali, who reigned from 1464 to 1491, stabilized the empire by making better laws and by expanding trade. Sonni Ali's forces conquered Tombouctou and Djenné, two important cultural and trading hubs in West Africa. The regime established its capital at Gao.

Sonni Ali's eventual successor, Askia Muhammad, brought the Songhai Empire to its peak in the early 1500s. Under his rule, the realm stretched from the Atlantic coast to Nigeria. It included most of the former Mali Empire. The government efficiently managed the richest domain in West Africa. The emperor encouraged his subjects to adopt Islam. He restored Tombouctou as an important Islamic center.

The sons of Askia Muhammad forced him to give up his throne in 1528. Afterward, the empire declined as they fought one another for control. Outsiders saw the realm's internal weakness as an opportunity to invade. The Songhai Empire survived several clashes until 1591. In that year, the Moroccan leader Ahmed al-Mansur attacked with heavily armed soldiers. Lacking equal force, the Songhai army was defeated near Gao in the Battle of Tondibi.

The Moroccans used places such as Tombouctou as outposts for the trade in gold and slaves that they conducted with ports on the Mediterranean Sea. In general, however, the Moroccans weakly governed the region.

◗ New Kingdoms, the Slave Trade, and the Spread of Islam

After the decline of the great empires, a number of small realms developed in central Mali. Among these domains were the Fulbé (also called Peul) kingdom of Macina (1400–1862) and the Bambara kingdoms of Ségou (1600–1862) and Kaarta (1663–1854). Initially, the wealth of these kingdoms came from raising livestock and farming the land. Later—partly in response to increasing European demands for slaves—the realms prospered by capturing and sending people to slave-trading stations on the Atlantic coast. To some extent, the kingdoms of Kaarta and Ségou were founded on the profits of slavery.

Throughout Africa and the Middle East, slave trading had been an ongoing economic activity for many centuries. Beginning in the late 1500s, however, European traders began to buy many more slaves. Plantation owners in new colonies in the Americas were demanding cheap labor. European buyers and the leaders of some African states saw the increased demand for slaves as a chance to make money. Raiders captured thousands of people in Mali. They

White plantation owners inspect African slaves during a sale. To learn more about the African slave trade, visit www.vgsbooks.com for links.

forced captives to walk to the coasts of present-day Senegal, Gambia, and Guinea.

Captives destined for American plantations became living cargo on slave ships. They traveled in dreadful conditions with large numbers of other Africans. Many died. Over the next three hundred years, millions of West Africans were enslaved under the Atlantic slave system. Not all the slaves from Mali ended up in the Americas. Some captives were sent to other African states, and some were sold to Middle Eastern markets.

As the Atlantic slave trade increased, the ancient caravan routes across the Sahara shifted eastward. Internal warfare and dwindling supplies of precious goods in the west were among the reasons for the shift. As a result, West Africa's waterways became major passageways for goods traded throughout the region. The shift to water routes benefited the Dyula, a people who managed much of the river traffic in West Africa. *Dyula* means "traders."

Most Dyula were Muslims. Their constant movement in search of trade brought the Islamic religion to a wider population. Another spur to the spread of Islam was the Fulbé kingdom, which supported jihads—religious struggles to convert non-Muslims to the religion.

By the 1700s, slave raids had driven Mali's Dogon, Bambara, and Senufo peoples from their villages. Wars and raids to capture slaves weakened African societies. Slave traders preferred healthy young men and women. The loss of these productive workers hurt local economies and families. During the 1700s in Europe, opposition to slavery grew among people who condemned it as cruel and inhuman.

◉ European Exploration and the 1800s

In the late-1700s, the Industrial Revolution in Europe saw the rise of power-driven machines. This fueled nations' economic and military forces. It also led to the demand for more natural resources for industry. Europeans increased their interest in foreign lands, such as West Africa, which could provide minerals, wood, cotton, and other raw materials.

One form of trade dwindled, however. In 1807 Britain outlawed the Atlantic slave trade. Other European nations soon followed. But slavery remained legal in the United States. As a result, slave traders continued the profitable business.

Coastal trade between Africa and Europe had occurred for centuries. But explorations to the African interior were rare until the early 1800s. Among Europeans, honor and fame could be won by making new discoveries. The first European to reach Malian territory and return alive was the Frenchman René-Auguste Caillié. He left North Africa in 1827, disguised as an Arab, and traveled across the Sahara to Tombouctou.

René-Auguste Caillié completed this drawing of Tombouctou in 1828.

Other European adventurers tried to map the course of the Niger River. The Scottish doctor Mungo Park was the first. Like others to come, he died in the attempt. In 1830 the British explorer Richard Lander and his brother John traced the waterway to the Gulf of Guinea. As Europeans charted more of the West African interior, their nations tried to establish colonial rule. Europeans wanted to control the source of natural resources instead of trading for them. Yet strong, advanced African states had long governed many parts of West Africa—particularly in Mali. They did not welcome European authority.

Christian missionaries, or religious teachers, also sought to spread their beliefs to what they saw as uncivilized and nonreligious cultures. Malian civilizations had their own belief systems, including Islam. Yet Christianity made some gains, especially in places where slave trading had undermined age-old cultures.

THE SILENCE OF TOMBOUCTOU

René-Auguste Caillié (1799–1838) was the first European to reach Tombouctou and return safely. Europeans did not realize that the legendary city of gold had declined since 1600. Caillié was disappointed when he got there. In his memoirs, *Travels through Central Africa to Timbuctoo, 1824–28*, Caillié described his impressions:

"I looked around and found that the sight before me did not answer my expectations. I had formed a totally different idea of the grandeur and wealth of Timbuctoo. The city presented, at first view, nothing but a mass of ill-looking houses, built of earth. Nothing was to be seen in all directions but immense plains of sand of a yellowish white color. The sky was a pale red as far as the horizon; all nature wore a dreary aspect, and the most profound silence prevailed; not even the warbling of a bird was to be heard."

In the mid-1800s, the Tall dynasty of the Tukulor realm subdued the various Malian kingdoms that had emerged after the fall of the Songhai Empire. Al-Hajj Umar was an Islamic scholar and skilled military commander. He founded the Tukulor realm as the result of a jihad that he launched in 1852. Umar gained a large following by preaching against what he thought were the corrupt practices of West African Muslims. In 1854 his troops conquered the Bambara kingdom of Kaarta (near present-day Nioro du Sahel, Mali). In 1862 they took Ségou and Macina. After Umar's death in 1864, his son, Amadou Tall, succeeded him in Ségou. Amadou's brother Muhammad Muntaga Tall ruled Kaarta, and their cousin Tijani Tall reigned over Macina.

Samory Touré and French Colonization

In the late 1800s, Samory Touré, a strong Malinke leader, established political control over much of southern Mali. With his capital at Bissandougou (part of Guinea), Samory attempted to reunite the former Mali Empire. His realm included the Bouré gold fields and the headwaters (the beginning of a river) of the Niger River (both in modern Guinea).

Following their explorations of Africa, European powers established colonial areas of influence on the continent. By the late 1800s, the European scramble for African colonies was intense. It endangered Mali's isolated position in the African interior.

France already had strong footholds in coastal areas of West Africa. French leaders decided to extend France's claims inland in the 1880s. They planned to build a trans-Saharan railroad to run through France's colonial empire in Africa to the Mediterranean Sea. The French soon established forts at Kita and Bamako. They completed a railway that reached from Dakar, Senegal, to Kayes and continued to the Niger River.

In order to fulfill their plans, the French began an all-out push for control of Mali. In 1887 they signed the Treaty of Bissandougou with Samory Touré. Under the agreement, the African ruler promised not to enlarge his domain north of the Niger River.

In 1889, however, Samory Touré rejected the treaty. For the next decade, he resisted France's efforts to expand its colonial holdings in West Africa. To secure his realm, Samory Touré also fought against other African kingdoms. He sold people into slavery to buy horses and weapons.

The Ségou kingdom of Amadou Tall surrendered to French troops in 1892. Six years later, the French captured Samory Touré. The fall from power of these two strong commanders signaled the end of African leadership in Mali for many decades. By 1900 the French flag was flying over an enormous section of Africa. France's holdings stretched from Senegal eastward to Lake Chad and northward to the Mediterranean Sea.

In 1904 France reorganized its territory in West Africa to form the Federation of French West Africa. This territory covered 1,789,186 square miles (4,633,970 sq. km), about half the size of the modern United States. By 1920 regional unrest and the need to divide the large federation into smaller units caused France to redraw the federation's boundaries to form eight colonies. Present-day Mali was called French Sudan (not related to the modern nation of Sudan). Senegal, French Guinea (modern Guinea), Dahomey (modern Benin), and Côte d'Ivoire (Ivory Coast) lost and gained territory. Upper Volta (modern Burkina Faso), Niger, and Mauritania composed the remainder of the new federation.

Colonial Rule

The governor of French Sudan ruled under the authority of the governor-general in Dakar, Senegal—the headquarters of French West African administration. The governor-general, in turn, took orders from the minister of colonies in France. This governmental framework had no place for Africans. In a few areas, such as Macina, Fulbé noble families maintained some power by accepting French authority. They collected taxes and provided workers for French building projects.

By the 1930s, a small number of French-educated interpreters, teachers, office workers, and doctors' assistants staffed part of the colonial administration in French Sudan. This African group was never more than 5 percent of the colony's total population. The rest of the people became the object of the French policy of "assimilation." The framers of this plan intended to absorb Africans into the greater French empire as French citizens. The program included imposing French education. It tried to break down traditional ethnic loyalties and to strengthen ties to France. But in reality, most Africans remained second-class subjects, not equal citizens of France.

In a further effort to make French Sudan into a more valuable French colony, France imposed other policies. Officials forced Africans to work without pay on public works projects, such as road building. The French also drafted men for military service. Much of the interior remained under French military control, and political activity was not permitted. Furthermore, the colonial legal system allowed people to be put in prison without trial. By the time World War II (1939–1945) broke out in 1939, Africans in French Sudan were ready for change.

World War II and Independence

France fell to the forces of Nazi Germany in 1940, and the Germans set up a pro-Nazi government in Vichy, France. A resistance movement—called Free France—began operating in exile under General Charles de Gaulle. French officials in Africa were faced with a difficult decision. The choice was whether to be loyal to the Vichy government or to join the Free France forces. The governor of French Sudan declared his loyalty to the Vichy government. Many Africans in French Sudan, however, chose to support de Gaulle and Free France. Some fled to the independent country of Liberia and to nearby British colonies to join the French war effort.

Hundreds of Africans from French Sudan served abroad in the armed forces of Free France. Within the colony, Africans grew rice and raised money to help the French resistance. In exchange for their participation, General de Gaulle promised the Africans in French Sudan a better life after the war. The experience of fighting for a common goal unified Bambara, Senufo, and Dogon troops. When they returned home, many of the soldiers had come to see themselves as part of an African nation rather than as members of separate ethnic communities. This realization fueled a growing nationalist movement. Nationalists sought self-rule for European colonies in Africa.

Allied armies liberated France in 1944, and the war ended in 1945. Afterward, France revised its colonial policies regarding Africa and created the French Union. This group had a national assembly whose voting membership was evenly divided between France and its overseas colonies. The new union outlawed forced labor and set up a federal council for all of French West Africa.

African Political Parties

Many Africans did not believe that France's view of the future was in their best interests. In 1946 West African leaders met in Bamako to found the continent's first interterritorial party—the Rassemblement Démocratique Africain (RDA, or African Democratic Rally). Under party leader Modibo Keita, the new organization expressed the colony's growing desire for independence.

The French Union lasted until 1956, when African efforts resulted in some reforms, including more self-government for French Sudan. In 1957 another RDA conference was held in Bamako. This time, however, disputes among party members emerged. Keita and his colleagues viewed the RDA's cooperation with France as an attempt to weaken nationalist movements. These leaders broke with the RDA.

Soon afterward, France again reorganized several of its overseas holdings, offering them independence within a newly formed French Community. Along with Senegal, French Sudan voted for self-rule within the French Community in 1958. In 1959 the two nations combined to form the Mali Federation. Keita served as prime minister. The leaders hoped the federation would bring economic and social benefits to both countries.

Modibo Keita was independent Mali's first president. He was born in Bamako in 1915 and died there in 1977.

Political disagreements between the former colonies caused the Mali Federation to break up in August 1960. On September 22, 1960, Keita proclaimed the founding of the independent Republic of Mali. He became its first president. The new state withdrew from the French Community. Soon after, Mali also abandoned the franc zone—an economic group that used the French franc as a common form of money. For a brief time, Mali associated itself with Guinea and Ghana, but this union dissolved in 1963.

Keita's Regime

In the 1960s, Keita and his Union Soudanaise (US) Party attempted a bold program of state-funded social and economic development called socialism. The new plans were meant to make Mali independent of foreign influence. Keita called for the withdrawal of French soldiers stationed in Mali and demanded the return of Malian troops serving in the French armed forces. The president also halted France's testing of nuclear weapons in the Malian Sahara. Keita's economic agenda included plans for collectivization—that is, combining many small farms to increase agricultural production.

France, which had better relations with its other former colonies than with Mali, chose not to trade its goods with Mali. To overcome this and other economic difficulties, Mali turned for aid to the governments of the Soviet Union (a former union of republics including Russia) and China. These countries were Communist, with economies controlled by the state, not private businesspeople. Pro-French businesspeople disliked the Communist system, which affected their ability to move goods. As a result, the availability of consumer goods declined. These events led to unrest as Keita's regime became less able to meet the needs of ordinary Malians.

In 1967 Keita announced measures to combat the country's severe economic problems. The public, however, was reluctant to endure the hardships that Keita's economic programs had caused. That year Keita also launched a cultural revolution to rid the US Party of people who opposed his ideas. Widespread removals of party officials followed at all levels. To further frighten his rivals, Keita increased the power of the Popular Militia—an armed branch of the US Party. The president also dissolved the National Assembly.

The Popular Militia became a brutal force throughout the country. Keita and his government lost support as arrests and torture created strong grassroots opposition. The Popular Militia's increasing size and its harassment of the national army motivated some army officers, led by Moussa Traoré, to act. On November 19, 1968, they overthrew the Keita regime and imprisoned Keita.

Mali under Traoré

Traoré's leadership of the November overthrow established him as chief of state. In 1969 Traoré became president of Mali.

Severe droughts that resulted in poverty and famine plagued the nation in the 1970s. Public dissatisfaction with the Traoré regime rose. Nevertheless, the president survived attempts of various army factions to overthrow his government. In 1976 President Traoré founded

Nomads linger near a dried-up river in Mali. Severe **drought** in the Sahel region crippled Mali in the 1970s. Without fresh water to drink, millions of livestock died. Fulani and Tuareg herders, who rely on livestock for meat and milk, died also from malnutrition.

the Democratic Union of the Malian People (UDPM). Supposedly civilian (nonmilitary), it included many military supporters of Traoré. The regime allowed no opposition parties and put down dissent with arrests and torture. In 1978 and 1980, opponents tried but failed to dislodge Traoré. A trans-Saharan drought in 1984 again devastated the nation, but in 1985, a majority of voters reelected Traoré.

By the early 1990s, however, dissatisfaction with the corrupt Traoré government and demands for democracy had grown. In March 1991, while students, workers, and other prodemocracy rioters paralyzed the capital, members of the Malian armed forces arrested Traoré and overthrew the government. The coup leader, Amadou Toumani Touré, then announced plans for Mali's first multiparty elections. Touré won popularity for returning Mali to civilian rule.

Transition to Democracy

In 1992 Malians voted for Alpha Oumar Konare to be Mali's first freely elected president. Konare's party, Alliance for Democracy in Mali (ADEMA), won a majority in the legislature (lawmaking body).

Konare's government struggled with economic and military problems. Measures to reduce government spending sparked violent protests among Malian students in 1993 and 1994. Mali also faced rebellions by Tuareg people on its northern borders. This distinct ethnic group has long wanted independence from southern Mali. Malian armed forces fought with several different Tuareg rebel groups based in southern Algeria. To escape the violence, thousands of Malian refugees fled to Algeria, Mauritania, and Burkina Faso. The government eventually agreed to allow more self-rule for northerners and to increase government spending in the poor north.

In 1996 a public ceremony called Flamme de la Paix (peace flame) in Tombouctou celebrated a peace agreement between the fighting parties. Thousands of refugees returned home. Most of Mali's other ethnic groups get along peacefully together.

Into the Twenty-First Century

Voters reelected Konare to his second term in 1997. According to the constitution, it would be his last term. At the next presidential election, in 2002, more than twenty-four candidates ran for president. Amadou Toumani Touré, the man who had overthrown the regime of Traoré, emerged the winner with 64 percent of the vote.

Mali, a very poor country, has borrowed a lot of money from other countries. It struggles to pay off a foreign debt of more than $3 billion. President Touré met with French president Jacques Chirac in 2002. Afterward, France announced that it would cancel 40 percent of Mali's

President Amadou Toumani Touré is popularly known as ATT. He has also earned the nickname soldier of democracy for letting elected civilians run much of the country. This approach is a big change from the military dictatorship of Touré's predeccesor, Moussa Traoré.

debt to France, amounting to about $79 million. But that same year, refugees from civil conflict in Ivory Coast added to the drain on Mali's limited resources.

The next year, the International Monetary Fund (the IMF, a United Nations agency) canceled another $675 million of Mali's debt. This debt relief is part of the Heavily Indebted Poor Countries (HIPC) Initiative. This plan aims to help the world's poorest countries like Mali improve basic social services and stand on their own.

In the early twenty-first century, Mali's political stability offers hope that the country will move forward. President Touré does not belong to a political party. His "government of national unity" includes representatives from a broad range of Malian political points of view. National goals include encouraging trade, developing industry and roads, and improving educational and health systems. The moderate Islamic country also participates in the global war on terrorism. The Malian military works with the United States in the Trans-Sahara Plan. This plan coordinates efforts to find and shut down terrorist camps in the Sahara.

In 2003 former president Konare became chair of the African Union (AU). The AU is an organization formed in 2002. Its membership of fifty-three African nations promotes democracy, peace and security, and foreign investment in Africa.

But Mali still has many problems. Drought and a locust plague in 2004 reduced Mali's cereal harvest by as much as 45 percent. The UN's World Food Program reports that severe food shortages threaten the lives and health of one million Malians.

In 2006 the city of Bamako hosted the first African meetings of the World Social Forum (WSF). About twenty thousand people came from around the world. Founded in Brazil in 2001, the WSF is an organization of citizens' groups, mainly from poor countries. It aims to empower developing nations to fight poverty, disease, and pollution. The WSF supports local solutions and the right of developing countries to decide their own future.

Government

After the overthrow of the Traoré government, Malian officials wrote a new constitution, which established the Third Republic of Mali. This 1992 constitution provides for a multiparty state and popularly elected representatives. All citizens eighteen years and older have the right to vote.

Every five years, Malians elect a president with a limit of two terms. The president holds executive power as head of state. The president selects a prime minister who has responsibility for the day-to-day operations of the government. The prime minister appoints a Council of Ministers, or cabinet, which includes the heads of sixteen government ministries.

Mali's legislature is a unicameral (one-chamber) body of 147 members called the National Assembly. Elections for lawmakers, like those for president, take place every five years. The legislature includes thirteen seats for representatives of Malians living abroad. In 2006 sixteen political parties were represented in the National Assembly.

Mali's judicial system, an arm of the executive branch, is based on France's legal code. New laws are drafted to reflect Malian life. The Supreme Court in Bamako is the highest court in the Malian justice system. A court of appeals also holds sessions in the capital. Beneath these national courts are regional courts and local courts, headed by justices of the peace.

For administrative purposes, Mali is divided into eight regions and the capital district of Bamako. Each is under the rule of an appointed governor. The eight regions are further divided into 46 *cercles* (sectors) and 279 *arrondissements* (districts). Elected mayors run city councils.

To learn more about Mali's history and government, including key political figures and colonial rule, visit www.vgsbooks.com.

THE PEOPLE

With 13.4 million inhabitants, Mali has an average of 28 people per square mile (11 per sq. km). This figure is one of the lowest population densities in West Africa, which averages 112 people per sq. mile (43 per sq. km). Yet the Malian population is distributed very unevenly. The highest concentrations are in the south. More than 2 million Malians live and work outside the country. Most move to France or nearby West African states. More men than women leave the country. The money they send back helps support their families.

Like most other African countries, Mali has a small urban population. Roughly 30 percent of the people live in cities. In addition, most Malians are very young—about 48 percent are under the age of 15. Only 3 percent live to be older than 65. The nation's high birthrate and short life expectancy (48 years) help explain the large percentage of youthful Malians. The average Malian woman gives birth to 7 children in her lifetime, the third-highest fertility rate in the world. As young people come into childbearing years, Mali's population growth is

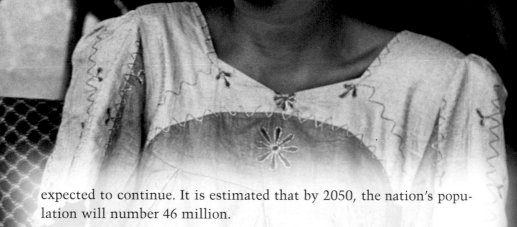

expected to continue. It is estimated that by 2050, the nation's population will number 46 million.

Ethnic and Language Groups

As an age-old crossroads of trade, Mali contains a variety of African
peoples and languages. Several large ethnic groups and a number of
smaller communities share one nation. Many of these societies have
common cultural and language ties, while others are quite distinct.
Except for ethnic tensions between northerners and southerners,
Mali's different groups generally live and work together in harmony.
Marriages between people of different groups are common.

The Bambara, Malinke, and Soninke peoples are all part of the Mande
language family (a group of related languages). All the Mande languages
are tonal. That is, they are pronounced with high, middle, or low tones.
The three groups together make up 50 percent of Mali's population. The
nation's single largest ethnic group is the Bambara, who live mostly in

MALINKE PROVERBS

Kuno se lii, naanaa mee lii.
"Your hair can be styled however you like, your future cannot."

Moxo mee i buloo bula saanaa to.
"A person should not put their hands in snake's poison." (Meaning, don't take useless risks.)

Kuma se mee daa fula le to.
"In two mouths, conversation lives long." (Meaning, honesty between two people is the foundation of friendship.)

the middle Niger River valley. The Bambara generally farm the land to make a living. Along with French, Mali's official language, people throughout the country widely understand the Bambara language.

Closely related to the Bambara are the Malinke of southwestern and western Mali. Their name means "the people of [the ancient empire of] Mali." They are also known as Mandinka. As heirs of the Mali Empire, the Malinke are proud of their history and traditions. Since ancient times, a special class of people called griots have been the traditional Malinke oral historians. Many Malinke are farmers or the recent descendants of farmers. The group has supplied most of Mali's politicians and senior army officers since independence.

The third Mande-language group, the Soninke, make their homes in the northwestern Sahel. Their ancestors were founders of the Ghana Empire. Modern Soninke are successful traders in Mali. They enjoy a higher standard of living than many other Malians.

The Fulbé people and Tukulors live in the inland delta of the Niger River and speak Fulani. The groups' cattle-owning ancestors originally moved to Mali from homelands in the Senegal River valley. Although both groups together make up only about 20 percent of the population, they

Many **Fulbé** women wear large gold earrings called *kwotenai kanye*. Only the wealthiest Fulbé wear the earrings, which are so heavy that the top of each earring must be wrapped in red fabric to protect the ear. Fulbé are also fond of tattoos, and many women tattoo the skin around their mouths.

A **Tuareg** husband and wife ride a camel. Many Tuareg are very proud of their North African heritage and consider themselves superior to other Malians. Among the Tuareg, men veil their faces and women do not.

claim superiority over other peoples because of their livestock-based wealth. The Fulbé and the Tukulors also take special pride in the role that their communities have played in Mali's history.

The Songhai (also spelled Songhay) make up 7 percent of Mali's population. They have a deep respect for their ancestors and their ancient traditions from the days of the Songhai Empire. Farming in the rural areas around Djenné and trading in the cities are ways of life for the Songhai. The market in Djenné is an important trade center for the region.

The Tuareg are the descendants of North African Berbers. They maintain a separate lifestyle in the Malian Sahara. Along with other desert nomads, they compose 5 percent of Malians. The Tuareg roam with their herds across international boundaries and are found in several countries. However, the droughts of the 1970s forced many Tuareg to give up their nomadic lifestyle. While most Malians are dark-skinned, the northern desert-dwelling Tuareg are light-skinned. They follow their own traditional leaders and see themselves as separate from the southerners. Therefore the group has long opposed the Malian government. Tuareg speak Tamaschek, an ancient Berber tongue, and use their own form of writing.

Several smaller ethnic groups make up most of the remaining population of Mali. Among these are the Gur-speaking Dogon. Their art forms, especially masks and statues, enjoy worldwide fame. Tourists travel to Dogon Country to see the villages built into colorful cliffs and to watch performances of masked dancers. But many young Dogon leave Mali for jobs in other nations. Additional members of Mali's African mixture

Dogon children ham it up for the camera. The Dogon are famous for their mythology and elaborate artwork. For more information about Mali's ethnic groups, visit www.vgsbooks.com for links.

include other peoples that speak the Gur language, such as the Senufo and the Bobo.

Few non-Africans live permanently in Mali. A small French community resides in the country as a result of commercial, educational, and administrative ties that began in colonial times. The Europeans, as well as Malian government workers, speak French. A limited number of Arabs, mostly dwelling in Bamako and in a few large towns, are involved in trade. They mainly speak Arabic.

◉ Daily Life and Women's Roles

Most Malians make their homes in small villages in the central savanna area and depend on the land for a living. People in rural areas follow ways of life that are much the same as their ancestors'. Malian farmers usually don't have modern machines. Using hand tools, they are able to produce little more than they need to feed their own families—a situation called subsistence farming.

Each village is made up of a cluster of straw-roofed houses made of sun-baked mud bricks. The dwellings are grouped into family compounds, which usually shelter extended families. Extended families include grandparents, aunts, and uncles, as well as parents, brothers, and sisters. Since Islamic law allows

CLOTHING

People in Mali's cities often wear European-style clothing. Men wear trousers, not shorts, and shirts. A long embroidered flowing robe called a *boubou* may be worn on top. Women are more likely to wear traditional clothes. They dress in long wraparound skirts, blouses, and sandals. Colorful, patterned cloth is popular. Women often wrap their heads with bright scarves.

A typical Malian **village** consists of mud-brick homes with straw roofs. A majority of Mali's population live in homes like these.

men to marry up to four wives, Malian families can become quite large. Some villages are made up of one large extended family. Elders make decisions for the group, such as which part of the village land is to be cultivated by each family group.

The ways of ordinary Malians are in sharp contrast to the lifestyles of the nation's relatively small wealthy class. These French-speaking citizens live in Bamako and in the larger regional towns. Most of them are members of the civil service (have government jobs) or engage in business. They hold most of the nation's wealth and power.

Despite laws to give women equal rights, Mali remains a patriarchal (male-ruled) society. Men hold most of the power in public life. Girls are less likely to receive an education than boys. Women make up only 10 percent of Mali's parliament. In 2006 five of the twenty-eight ministers are women.

But Malian women play an important role in the family and in providing food and income. They run stalls in outdoor markets. Rural women sow and harvest crops. They shoulder other heavy responsibilities, such as gathering

A traditional saying in Mali states, "Behind every beard you can see the tip of a braid." This reflects the situation that while men have public power, women often have a lot of influence behind the scenes.

firewood, cooking over a fire, carrying water, and doing the family's laundry by hand. They often walk with a load of wood or a container of water balanced on their heads. Mothers often carry their babies on their backs while they work. Women also have the daily task of preparing flour by pounding grain with long wooden poles. This work damages their hands.

As more and more men leave their villages to find work in cities or in other countries, women are left with more responsibilities. Malian women seek new ways to help themselves, their families, and their communities. Some women learn to read and write in adult literacy classes. Small credit plans and training programs offer women the opportunity to develop and run small businesses. Marketplaces are centers where women sell their produce and goods and meet to organize and socialize. Women are starting to find nontraditional jobs in urban areas too.

Almost all of Mali's young girls, from all ethnic groups, undergo excision, also called female genital mutilation (FGM). This is the practice of cutting away some or all of a girl's external genitalia and sewing the vagina mostly closed. It is estimated that more than 90 percent of Malian women have been excised. The cultural tradition continues, but as women become more educated, they are less likely to support FGM. Urban women are also less in favor of excision for their daughters than rural women are.

Malian women perform most of the daily chores, from doing laundry to pounding grain to make flour.

Anopheles **mosquito**

Health

Mali has some of the worst health statistics in the world. The average life expectancy in Mali is 48 years, compared to a world average of 67 years. Children are especially vulnerable to diseases caused by poor nutrition and poor sanitation. About 133 Malian babies out of every 1,000 die before they reach the age of 1. The world average infant mortality rate is 54 out of 1,000. A large percentage of Mali's children do not live to the age of 5. Only about 40 percent of births are attended by skilled medical workers. Women in Mali have a 1 in 10 chance of dying from childbearing causes.

A substantial number of Mali's people are poorly nourished. Malnutrition is one of the leading causes of children's death. Mothers who do not have good nutrition give birth to babies who are less healthy than well-nourished ones. The homes of most Malians also lack sanitary facilities. Without clean water, waterborne diseases such as diarrhea spread easily. Many young Malian children die from diarrhea.

Lack of trained medical personnel, particularly in rural areas, contributes to the poor health of most Malians. Few rural Malians receive adequate medical care. The country has an average of only one doctor for every 17,000 people and one sickbed for every 2,000 people. Health

MALARIA

Malaria is a dangerous disease common in warm and wet areas where mosquitoes breed, like southern Mali. The disease kills up to 3 million people around the world yearly. Protozoans (one-celled animals) called Plasmodia cause malaria. Spread by the bite of the female *Anopheles* mosquito, plasmodia from the mosquito's saliva enter a person's blood. They travel to the liver, where they multiply and form clumps of parasites. After several days, these clumps burst and release new plasmodia, which invade red blood cells. The infected blood cells eventually break open and release large numbers of plasmodia. This invasion continues, causing periodic fevers of 106°F (41°C). Attacks last about two hours and recur every two or three days. Headache, muscle pain, and nausea accompany the temperature swings. There are four types of malaria. Only one causes death if untreated. The other three retreat, even if untreated, but may recur periodically throughout a person's lifetime.

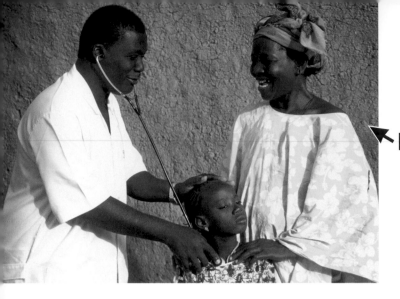

A doctor examines a child. Very few people in Mali receive adequate **health care.**

clinics are understaffed and poorly supplied. Even hospitals in major cities have inadequate supplies. Drought and famine have further complicated the health situation. Tuberculosis, influenza, and cholera cause frequent sickness. Rabies and measles are also present in Mali. Blindness is common, caused by trachoma, an easily spread bacterial eye disease. The rate of HIV/AIDS in the adult population is about 2 percent, or more than 100,000 people.

Parasites—organisms that feed on people, plants, and animals—cause many diseases in Mali. Bloodsucking insects such as mosquitoes, flies, and ticks pick up and transmit dangerous parasites when they feed on their victims. This is how malaria, typhus, sleeping sickness, and yellow fever are spread. Blackflies live in water, and their bites cause river blindness. This eye disease can lead to blindness. Schistosomiasis, also called bilharziasis, is a widespread and sometimes fatal disease caused by parasites in freshwater snails. The parasites enter the skin of people who go into the waters to wash, fish, or swim. Another kind of parasite destroys the lining of the intestines, causing a painful disease called amebic dysentery. Guinea worm, also in water, infects the skin.

Health authorities try to prevent these parasitic diseases by improving sanitation methods, reducing parasite-carrying animals, and educating people. Sometimes simple remedies are effective. For instance, filtering water removes guinea worm. Mosquito nets around beds and screens on windows reduce malaria. Worldwide, scientists are also working on a vaccine to prevent malaria.

◉ Education

Mali has a long heritage of educational achievement. Islamic schools date back to the thirteenth century, when teachers at Gao, Tombouctou, and Djenné attracted Muslim students throughout North Africa. Only males received education, however, as girls were considered mentally inferior.

Visit www.vgsbooks.com for links to websites with additional information about the people of Mali, including languages, daily life, health care, and education.

As early as 1887, the French colonial government established schools for the sons of Muslim leaders. At these institutions, pupils learned the French language and absorbed French culture. Graduates helped to fill the colonial administration's labor needs.

Since independence, Mali has attempted to improve public education. In the 1960s, the government spent more than 20 percent of its budget on education, and the number of classrooms and students increased rapidly. In the early 2000s, however, only 62 percent of children attend primary school, with far more boys than girls attending. The majority of adult Malians cannot read and write a basic sentence. Only 46 percent of the entire population is literate. Unequal literacy rates between the sexes—53 percent of men but only 40 percent of women are literate—reflects women's lower status in society.

Although the state funds most educational programs, Roman Catholic religious orders run a number of elementary and adult schools. Since Mali has no national university, some Malians study abroad, especially in France. College studies, similar to those offered at two-year community colleges in the United States, are available to the small percentage of the population that has enough money and political influence to gain access to further schooling.

Islamic school students learn the Quran, the Islamic holy book. Nearly 90 percent of the nation practices Islam.

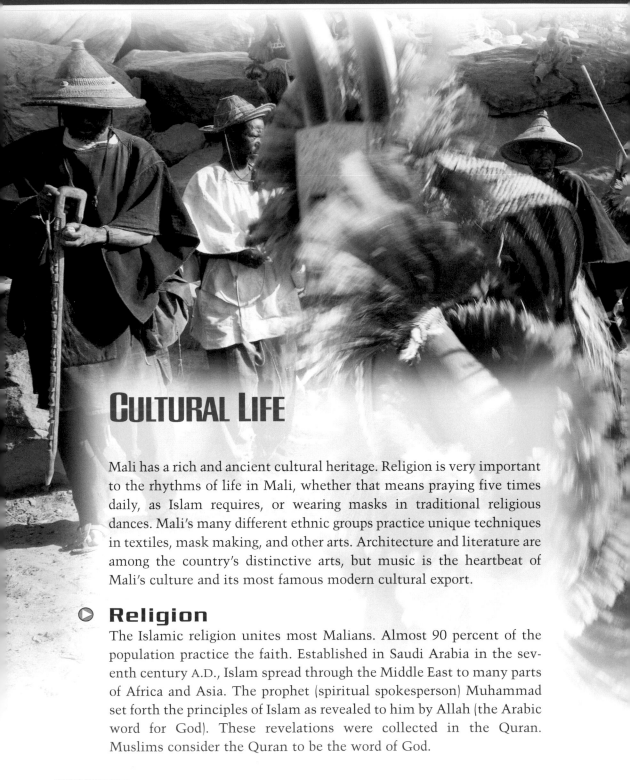

CULTURAL LIFE

Mali has a rich and ancient cultural heritage. Religion is very important to the rhythms of life in Mali, whether that means praying five times daily, as Islam requires, or wearing masks in traditional religious dances. Mali's many different ethnic groups practice unique techniques in textiles, mask making, and other arts. Architecture and literature are among the country's distinctive arts, but music is the heartbeat of Mali's culture and its most famous modern cultural export.

Religion

The Islamic religion unites most Malians. Almost 90 percent of the population practice the faith. Established in Saudi Arabia in the seventh century A.D., Islam spread through the Middle East to many parts of Africa and Asia. The prophet (spiritual spokesperson) Muhammad set forth the principles of Islam as revealed to him by Allah (the Arabic word for God). These revelations were collected in the Quran. Muslims consider the Quran to be the word of God.

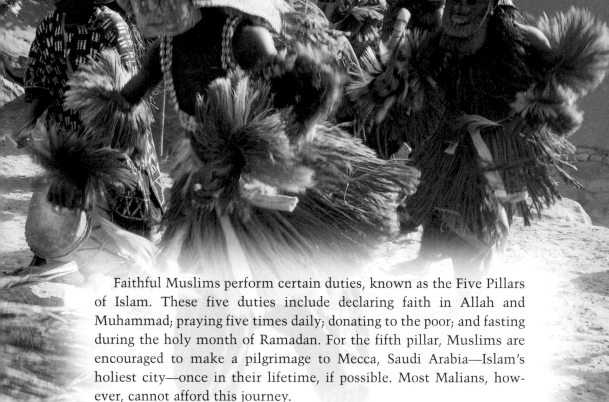

Faithful Muslims perform certain duties, known as the Five Pillars of Islam. These five duties include declaring faith in Allah and Muhammad; praying five times daily; donating to the poor; and fasting during the holy month of Ramadan. For the fifth pillar, Muslims are encouraged to make a pilgrimage to Mecca, Saudi Arabia—Islam's holiest city—once in their lifetime, if possible. Most Malians, however, cannot afford this journey.

Some Malian Muslims follow Islamic *tariqas*—powerful religious brotherhoods. These are often mystical, meaning they teach practices that seek to bring a believer closer to God. These organizations, such as the Tijani and the Qadiri brotherhoods, also wield political influence because they often control how their followers vote. But Malians in general do not seek to make Islam a political force, preferring to keep religion and state separate.

About 9 percent of Malians continue to practice traditional African beliefs (sometimes called animism). These religions take

THE DOGON'S BIG BANG THEORY

The traditional religion of the Dogon people is very complex. According to their creation story, in the beginning of time, a tiny seed floated in the empty darkness of space. Though extremely small, it contained everything, living and nonliving, that exists in the universe. Strong vibrations inside the seed caused it to explode suddenly. Everything in the seed, all the stars and planets, spread out to the edges of the universe. This ancient story is very like the big bang theory that modern science uses to explain the origins of the universe. According to this theory, the universe began billions of years ago. All matter was condensed to a size smaller than an atom. A violent explosion caused the matter to expand through the universe.

many different forms, but almost all focus on a universal life force in nature and natural events. Trees, rocks, wind, animals, people—all things have this life force, or spirit. Most traditional African religions also teach a belief in a supreme God, or Creator. Believers seek to control spiritual power for practical ends, such as to avoid sickness, secure a good job, or reap a big harvest. Often ancestors play a big role in contacting the spirit world. Ceremonies, rituals, and prayer, usually through a holy man or holy woman, are employed to ask for the ancestors' help. Music, dance, and masks are important aspects of these religions.

As a result of French influence, 1 percent of Malians follow Christianity, mostly Roman Catholicism. Protestantism is growing due to the efforts of missionary groups who operate schools and social welfare programs. Colonialism, the spread of Islam and Christianity, and modern ways have led to the decline of traditional religions. However, elements of ancient ways are sometimes blended into Muslim and Christian practices. This religious blending is called syncretism.

◉ The Arts

Malian artists focus their creative energies on making wood, metal, and cloth goods. European-influenced artists create watercolor and oil paintings. Self-trained artisans fashion wall paintings that depict scenes from daily life. Mali's architecture, as seen in the mud-based plaster mosque at Djenné, is world famous. Mali's rural architecture is an ongoing activity among community members because the buildings' mud plaster is worn away by wind and rain and needs constant restoration.

Masks in West African societies are used for ceremonial and religious purposes. They are not meant to stand alone like statues in museums. Rather, they are worn at special times, such as harvesttime or coming-of-age ceremonies. Mask making is found among settled farming groups. Mask makers are respected artists. Most masks are made of wood. Accompanied by music and dance, masks allow the wearers to take on an identity from the spirit world. One of the most famous and beautiful masks is Tyi Wara, the antelope who is believed to have taught farming to the original Bambara people. Modern Bambara are mostly Muslim. But in rural communities, farmers wearing Tyi Wara headdresses dance at planting time.

The Bambara people have also been making *bogolan*, or "mud cloth," for many generations. *Bogo* means "mud," and *lan* means "traces of." Bogolan makers paint symbolic designs on cotton cloth using mud that has natural mineral dyes in it. Chris Seydou, a Malian fashion designer in the 1990s, introduced the patterns of bogolan to the international fashion industry, where they gained popularity.

The Fulbé people also have a cloth-making tradition. Their most important weavings are wool blankets called *khasa*. Khasa are up to 8 feet (2.5 m) long, with red and black patterns on white. Herders who camp out in the desert with their animals use these blankets.

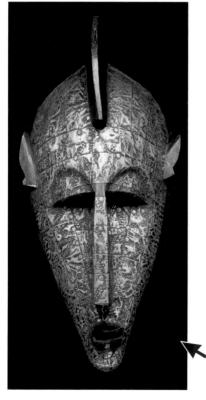

Many different art forms flourish in Mali. **Mask making** and **weaving** are both common. To learn more about art in Mali, visit www.vgsbooks.com for links.

◎ Literature and Communications

Mali has a long tradition of storytelling, and there are many traditional Malian folktales. Until the late 1500s, Islamic writers in Tombouctou and other former centers of learning produced important works of scholarship in Arabic, the traditional language of Islam and the Quran. In the 1800s, colonial rule introduced the French language into Mali. In 1923 language and folklore scholar Moussa B. Travélé published *Proverbes et contes Bambara* (Bambara Proverbs and Tales) in French. Until the 1950s, however, most Malians preferred to write in Arabic.

Mali has produced some important nonfiction and fiction writers. Most write in French. Amadou Hampate Ba published his first collection of poems in the 1950s. He is one of Mali's best-known authors. Ba's work brings together many traditional Malian oral legends, sayings, and folk stories. Published in 1955, *La Passion de Djimé (Djimé's Passion)* by Fily Dabo Sissoko was one of Mali's first novels. Available in English, *God's Bits of Wood* (1960) by Ousmane Sembene tells the story of the Africans who built the Dakar-Niger Railway. Djibril Tamsir Niane has written the story of Sundiata, the founder of the Mali Empire, in the Malinke language. In the countryside, people still recite ancient poems and ballads. Author Baba Wagué Diakité grew up in a Malian village hearing these tales told in the evenings around a fire. He moved to the United States. His children's books in English, such as *The Magic Gourd* (2003), retell some of these stories. They often involve magic elements, speaking animals, and teaching lessons.

Women writers from Mali, though few, produce some of the most important literary works in West Africa. Their work, usually written in French, is often difficult to find outside that region. Aoua Keita's themes include the life of women in Mali under French rule. Adame Ba

BROTHER RABBIT (DOGO ZAN)

In *The Magic Gourd* (2003), author Baba Wagué Diakité retells the folktale he heard growing up in Mali. Once, during a time of famine, Brother Rabbit (Dogo Zan) rescued Chameleon from a thorn bush. In thanks, Chameleon gave him a hollow gourd that magically filled with whatever its owner wanted. Rabbit used it to feed his hungry family and neighbors. But a greedy king came and took the gourd away. He used it only to make gold and food for himself. Chameleon then gave Rabbit a magic stone, which hit the king until he returned the gourd. Because Rabbit kindly let the king keep his gold and food, though, the king began to see the importance of friendship and sharing.

Konare's book *Ces mots que je partage: Discours d'une Première Dame d'Afrique* (These Words That I Share: Speeches by an African First Lady) is a collection of the speeches she delivered in the 1990s, when her husband was president of Mali. Fanta-Taga Tembley's novel *Dakan* (Destiny) was published in 2002.

Filmmakers have a hard time overcoming Mali's limited resources to make and distribute films. Nonetheless, Mali has produced a small number of important films. Soulemane Cisse is Mali's leading film director. His 1987 film *Yeelen* (Brightness) was the first African film ever to win awards at the international film festival in Cannes, France. Available with English subtitles, it is a historical fantasy about a young man with magical powers. Director Cheik Oumar Sissoko makes films that tell stories about poverty and injustice. His film *Le Vent* (The Wind) is about student opposition to President Traoré's regime. Abderrahmane Sissako filmed *Life on Earth* in Sokolo, Mali. It is available with English subtitles. This movie follows a man returning from Paris to visit his father in Mali for the beginning of the year 2000. But he sees that nothing has changed for Mali with the new millennium. The film captures the slow pattern of life and the dignity of people as they face drought and poverty. Foreign filmmakers have made documentaries about Mali, including *The Art of the Dogon* (1988).

Radios are the main way of getting information in villages, where many people may not be able to read. In addition, electricity is not always available, and televisions are very rare. Mali's news reporting is less restricted by censorship than most places in Africa. Mali has dozens of privately owned and state-run newspapers. Two daily national newspapers, both in French, are available in large towns. Mali's phone system is unreliable but improving. Villagers usually use the local post office to make calls. There are 56,000 landlines, and 250,000 people use cell phones. Only 25,000 people use the Internet in Mali.

Music

Music is a major art form that flourishes in Mali. Music is everywhere, from traditional music in villages to African pop music in big-city nightclubs. Talented players establish dance bands in towns. These groups use modern electronic equipment and play popular tunes drawn from all over the world. Much Malian music reflects the tradition of the griot. Ancient griots were royal storytellers, but present-day griots mix tales and music for the enjoyment of ordinary people. A griot often strums a kora, a twenty-one-stringed instrument, and may be accompanied by a musician playing a *balaphon* (a wooden xylophone).

There are many famous Malian musicians and singers, and some are known around the world. Salif Keita is the most famous singer in the Mande style, which is reserved for people of the ancient griot class. At first, Keita faced disapproval from all sides because he is not of this class. By 1987, however, his album *Soro* had become one of the best-selling African records ever. He favors slow-moving melodies. Keita moved to Paris, France, where there is a vibrant African music scene. He returns to Mali regularly for inspiration.

Oumou Sangaré is Mali's best-known female musician. Known as the Songbird of Wassoulou, she comes from a family of singers who perform music from the Wassoulou region. Most Wassoulou singers are women. Their themes include love, tradition, and the position of women in society. The music is based on ancient hunters' songs and songs of praise. Traditional instruments accompany the music, including the *fle*, a gourd draped

ROOTS OF THE BLUES

Ali Farka Touré (1949–2006) was a legendary blues guitarist and singer from northern Mali. He earned his nickname Farka, which means "donkey," because he stubbornly clung to life after his nine siblings all died in childhood. He said that the spirits gave him his musical gifts. Many listening to the pulsing, spellbinding power of his music find that easy to believe. American blues music has its roots in West Africa, brought by enslaved people to the Americas. Some people have compared the great bluesman from Mississippi, John Lee Hooker, to Touré. Touré released the last of many albums, *In the Heart of the Moon*, in 2005.

In 2006 **Toumani Diabaté** won a Grammy for Best Traditional World Music Album for his work (with Ali Farka Touré) on *In the Heart of the Moon*.

with cowrie shells, which the singers twirl and rhythmically toss into the air. Sangaré blends Wassoulou dance rhythms with mainstream musical styles. Her songs promote woman's rights. Sangaré especially opposes polygamy (having multiple wives), because she saw the negative effect the practice had on her mother.

Sports, Recreation, and Holidays

By far the favorite sport in Mali is soccer, called football. The most popular national teams are Djoliba, Stad, and Real, but many people also support British and French teams. Young people often play informal games, with a bundle of rags for a soccer ball, in the cool of the evening. The country's most famous soccer player is Salif Keita (not the musician of the same name). He established a school for young soccer players to encourage new talent. In 2002 Mali was proud to host the all-Africa soccer tournament called the African Cup of Nations. Basketball is also very popular in Mali, with several national competitions.

Malians play *wari*, a version of a board game that people all over Africa have played for thousands of years. It is known by many different names, such as mancala. The board is rectangular, with two rows of six carved cups each. Two players move counters around the board trying to capture each other's counters. If there is no board available, people scoop cups into the dirt and play with stones.

A group of young boys plays a quick game of football on the playing field in their village.

Residents of Tombouctou repair the city's **Djinguereber Mosque** in preparation for the Maouloud festival, which celebrates the birth of Muhammad. Mansa Musa had the mosque built in the early 1300s after returning from a pilgrimage to Mecca.

The month of Ramadan is the most important Muslim holiday, when people fast during the day in honor of Allah revealing Islam to Muhammad. Islam follows a lunar (moon) calendar, so dates of Islamic holidays change every year. Secular (nonreligious) holidays in Mali include New Year's Day (January 1) and Independence Day (September 22). Local communities hold annual celebrations at times of agricultural importance, such as planting and harvesting. Festivities usually include dance and music.

"SWEET AS LOVE"

Malians serve tea by pouring it from a pot high above small glasses. The hot, sweet tea makes an arc through the air. It is tradition to refill the teapot three times and for everyone to drink three glasses of tea. The fresh-brewed first glass is said to be "strong as death." The second glass is "mild as life." And the third and final glass is "sweet as love."

◉ Food

Malian cuisine varies from region to region. But because food is often scarce, food choices are limited. Most Malians survive on a simple diet. Young girls learn from their mothers how to pound grain into flour, build a cooking fire, and prepare food. Most meals are based on a kind of porridge with a sauce. Millet (a grain), cassava (a root crop, also called manioc or tapioca), corn (called maize in Mali), rice, and beans provide the basic food for most Malians. *To* is a meal of millet porridge served with a

SESAME SEED STICKS (MENI-MENIYONG)

These sweets are sold in food stalls in marketplaces.

1 cup raw sesame seeds

4 tablespoons butter

1 cup sugar

1. Heat the sesame seeds at low heat in a shallow pan without any oil, until they begin to jump about and turn golden. Shake the pan so that they do not stick or burn. Remove from pan and let cool.
2. Melt the butter over low heat in a heavy pan. Add the sugar to the pan. Stir continuously until the sugar melts and the mixture turns slightly brown. Be careful: melted sugar is sticky and can burn you.
3. Add sesame seeds to the warm mixture. Mix well.
4. Transfer the mixture onto a cookie sheet lined with wax paper. When cool, shape it into sticks either by cutting or rolling. Coat sticks with more sesame seeds if they are too sticky.

sauce of meat or vegetables. Malians eat cassava raw, bake it in the embers of small fires, or soak it and grate it into flour. Cassava flour has little nutritional value, but it can be stored for weeks and is easy to transport.

Few Malians can afford to eat meat. In regions near rivers and streams, however, dried, fresh, or smoked fish sometimes is served at mealtimes. Wealthy urban dwellers, in contrast, often dine on chicken, goat, and beef, as well as fresh fruit and vegetables.

A meal in an urban restaurant or among the prosperous might consist of grilled beef; a salad of lettuce, tomatoes, and onions; and deep-fried strips of cassava, similar to french fries. Desserts include fresh melons, papayas, or mangoes. Other specialties are peanut-flavored chicken stew over rice and freshly caught Nile perch—called *capitaine* in Mali—served with a spicy sauce. Islam forbids Muslims to eat pork.

Tea is a common drink in Mali. Traditionally, three glasses of very sweet tea follow the evening meal. Coffee is not as popular and is mostly instant coffee. Islam forbids drinking alcohol, but homemade millet beer is available in Mali. Kola nuts are marble-sized nuts sold in markets. People chew these bitter nuts for their stimulating caffeine. Soft drinks are also available almost everywhere in Mali.

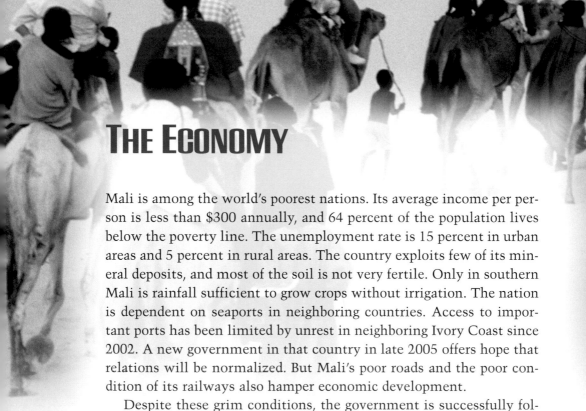

THE ECONOMY

Mali is among the world's poorest nations. Its average income per person is less than $300 annually, and 64 percent of the population lives below the poverty line. The unemployment rate is 15 percent in urban areas and 5 percent in rural areas. The country exploits few of its mineral deposits, and most of the soil is not very fertile. Only in southern Mali is rainfall sufficient to grow crops without irrigation. The nation is dependent on seaports in neighboring countries. Access to important ports has been limited by unrest in neighboring Ivory Coast since 2002. A new government in that country in late 2005 offers hope that relations will be normalized. But Mali's poor roads and the poor condition of its railways also hamper economic development.

Despite these grim conditions, the government is successfully following an economic reform program. Recommended by the International Monetary Fund, this plan includes privatization, or the selling of government-owned companies to private owners. The government's actions are helping the economy grow, attracting foreign

investment, and diversifying the economy. To diversify, the government encourages moving out of traditional, rural ways of life into an urban, industrialized society. This brings economic improvements to Mali. However, industrial development also creates challenges for developing countries like Mali. The changes may break down families and traditional lifestyles as people move to the cities for jobs. Industrial growth also creates more pollution. Mali seeks to balance its economic needs with protecting its environment and culture.

Like many developing countries, Mali struggles under the burden of paying off huge debts to many different foreign lenders. Mali's willingness to make IMF-recommended changes in recent years made it eligible for the Heavily Indebted Poor Countries Initiative. Money that used to go to pay debts to the IMF can instead pay for programs to reduce poverty in the country. Mali is also benefiting from debt forgiveness under a G8 (Group of 8) agreement. The G8 is an annual meeting of the world's eight most powerful countries, including the United States. Mali is using these plans to move toward self-sufficiency.

◉ Agriculture and Fishing

Although less than 10 percent of the country's land is suitable for crops, the Malian economy is based on agriculture. Agriculture, including farming crops, raising livestock, and fishing, provides 45 percent of the country's gross domestic product (GDP, the value of goods and services produced in a country in a year). Agriculture employs at least 80 percent of the country's workforce. After they feed their families, most farmers do not have any food left to sell at markets. Cotton and livestock are the major agricultural export earners, accounting for the majority of the nation's foreign income.

In the 1920s and 1930s, the French introduced two major cash (money-earning) crops—peanuts and cotton. With extensive irrigation, cotton can be planted in the south. Peanuts grow well in the west. Production of these cash crops has steadily increased, although market prices have varied. When world prices for Mali's export crops fall, farmers who rely on that income cannot afford to buy food.

Mali's best land is reserved for cash crops. Less-fertile plots are set aside for cassava and sorghum, which thrive in poor soil and need little care. As a result, many Malians are undernourished because the health-giving foods are sold, while poor crops form the basic Malian diet.

Droughts beginning in the 1970s have decreased yields of both cash crops and food items. Mali's poor transportation network limits the ability of farmers to get their crops and animals to a big, central market. The government made reforms in agriculture, and harvests began to rise in the early 2000s. In 2003–2004, cotton harvests were at record highs. But locust swarms in 2004 devastated cereal harvests. The country's food stocks are slowly recovering.

Most Malians cultivate the land much as their ancestors have for generations, using a slash-and-burn technique. Farmworkers clear away vegetation by cutting it down. The stubble of the plants is then burned—a process that also makes the soil fertile. After the plot has been planted, farmers use simple tools, such as hoes and animal-drawn plows, to tend the field. Rice and sugarcane are grown in central Mali. Millet, corn, and vegetables thrive in the south. Noncultivated items, such as edible oil from shea nuts, are almost as important as cultivated products in providing food to the population.

Cattle are raised throughout Mali, mostly by nomadic herding peoples, such as the Tuareg. Almost half of the animals belonging to the Tuareg died during the droughts of the 1970s and 1980s, eroding the Tuareg way of life. The herds are not expected to reach pre-drought levels again, due to the ongoing effect of drought. Herders raise sheep, goats, and camels in the north, as they do better than cattle in the dry areas. Cattle production has shifted to the south. Goats and sheep roam freely in most areas of the country, as do chickens, guinea fowls, turkeys, ducks, horses, and donkeys.

Mali's fishing industry is concentrated in the rivers and in a few lakes, particularly Lake Debo. The Niger alone contains over 180 species of fish, including carp, catfish, and perch. Fish follow the seasonal flood patterns of the rivers, and fishers live a seminomadic lifestyle in search of their daily catch. The government expanded the fishing industry by building small factories to store and package the

Men **fish** in the traditional way from a pirogue in the Niger River.

fish. However, due to drought and the drain of river water for crops, fish production has declined. The government is developing fish breeding plans to boost production.

The center of Mali's processing industry is Mopti, where workers process and market much of the nation's freshwater catch. Villagers along the banks of the rivers prepare fish for sale by smoking, drying, and salting them. These processed food products contribute significantly to Mali's foreign income. Most of the fish go to other countries in West Africa, particularly to Burkina Faso and Ivory Coast.

▶ Industry, Manufacturing, and Mining

Industry, including manufacturing and mining, provides 17 percent of Mali's GDP. Manufacturing activity mostly involves processing farm products. Rice-processing plants lie in the inland delta. A sugar refinery operates south of Bamako. The capital also has a number of industrial sites that produce ceramics, matches, cigarettes, leather, beer, and furniture. Mali's small industrial firms include textile factories, a cement plant, a peanut oil and soap complex, and a canning factory.

Mining is a growing industry in Mali. Gold makes up 80 percent of mining activity. In 2002 it briefly passed cotton and livestock to become Mali's main export earner. Two large companies mine gold in the western and southern parts of the country. Foreign investors own these companies. While gold is an important earner, the price of gold varies a lot on the world market. Earnings from such variable goods do not provide the stability Mali's economy needs.

In western Mali are considerable quantities of iron ore and bauxite (the raw material in aluminum). A relatively large deposit of phosphate lies in the Gao region and has encouraged a venture to mine this area. Mali also contains manganese and lithium reserves near Kayes and Bougouni. A marble deposit at Bafoulabé meets

THE HIGH PRICE OF GOLD

The price of gold in 2005 reached a peak of five hundred dollars an ounce (28 grams). The environmental cost of mining gold is also high. Much of the world's easily mined gold has already been used. Therefore, to extract 1 ounce of gold, enough for a ring, workers have to dig up 30 tons (27 metric tons) of rock. They pile up the rock and sprinkle it with diluted cyanide, a deadly chemical. This chemical solution separates the tiny amounts of gold from rock but also drains poison into the earth.

A man cuts slabs of salt into smaller tablets. Salt is still an important commodity in Mali that used to be traded for gold. The camel caravans that bring the salt out of the desert are among the last genuine working caravans in Africa.

local needs, and a large limestone quarry furnishes raw material for a cement factory.

Salt deposits at Taoudenni in northern Mali have been mined for at least one thousand years. About 5,000 tons (4,536 metric tons) of salt are removed annually from this remote area. Camels still carry much of the salt out of the desert, although four-wheel-drive vehicles are replacing them.

Services, Transportation, and Energy

The service sector of a country's economy provides services rather than producing goods. It includes jobs in government, health care, education, retail trade, banking, and tourism. The service sector provides 38 percent of Mali's GDP. Tourism is a small earner for Mali's economy, but it has a lot of potential. Niger River cruises, tours of the dramatic desert landscape, hiking in the Dogon Country, ancient cities, archaeological sites, and cultural festivals are all attractions for tourists. The government is improving the country's infrastructure, or system of public works such as roads, to increase the ease of travel in the country.

In general, most Malians rely on walking to get around. They often travel long distances on foot. Bicycles and mopeds are popular, as few Malians own cars. Mali has 9,383 miles (15,100 km) of roads, but 8,247 miles (13,273 km) of them are unpaved. Unpaved roads are passable

A **donkey cart** carries a family to market. Cars are very rare in Mali. Most people travel by foot.

most of the year, but some are washed out during the rainy seasons. Paved roads connect most major cities. A major paved highway connects Bamako to Mopti. This route opens the Dogon Country to tourism and makes it easier to transport fish to export markets.

The French laid the first railway lines in Mali in the late 1880s. More than a century later, the tracks stretch for 453 miles (729 km). Constant maintenance is required to keep trains running.

Transportation on the Niger River has improved in recent years. The waterway is navigable from Guinea to Niger between late August and January, depending on the rains. Boats can also travel on the Senegal River, where the Manantali Dam improved navigation in the early 1990s. This connection gives Mali part-time access to an Atlantic seaport—a major consideration for a landlocked, trade-dependent nation.

Mali has nine airports with paved runways and nineteen with unpaved runways. An international airport outside Bamako accommodates planes from other parts of West Africa and from Europe. Two privately owned air carriers handle domestic airline traffic on an irregular basis.

Hydroelectric power plants supply about half of Mali's electricity needs. These plants harness the power of rivers that flow in the southern part of the country. Imported petroleum fills much of the remainder of the nation's fuel requirements. The high price of petroleum and petroleum-based products uses a lot of Mali's limited money.

Visit www.vgsbooks.com for links to websites with additional information about Mali's economy. Convert U.S. dollars to CFA francs, learn about Malian agriculture and tourism, and more.

The Future

As a poor nation largely dependent on farming, Mali faces difficult challenges. Unpredictable harvests and long dry spells seriously affect the economy. In addition, inadequate food and unsafe water supplies endanger the health of Malians and disrupt traditional patterns of living.

Although Mali is poor economically, it is culturally rich. Music, literature, and art are expressions of the strong and vibrant people who are proud of their heritage. Mali has struggled with enormous difficulties but has held together as a nation.

In the twenty-first century, Mali's stable democratic government offers cautious hope for the future. Although the government attempts to address the basic needs of the people, much remains to be done to improve the Malian standard of living. The government of President Touré, elected in 2002, is committed to increasing economic growth, improving health and education, and strengthening democracy. It is also developing programs for counterterrorism and peacekeeping. These efforts attract international aid, which further enables Mali to address its challenges.

If the government and people of Mali continue to improve old social, economic, and political problems, Malians may yet escape the cycle of poverty and drought that has overshadowed their lives for decades. Then Malians will be able, as former president Konare said, to face their challenges and walk into the future on their own.

SENDING AID TO CANADA

An old Malian saying states, "If you cannot share the meager resources you have today, you will not know how to share the smallest part of your wealth tomorrow." In keeping with this wisdom, when ice storms badly damaged Saint Elizabeth, Canada, in 1998, the people of Sanankoroba, Mali, collected money to send to the Canadian farming community. Saint Elizabeth had sent Sanankoroba money when floods damaged that town a few years earlier. Moussa Konate, the Malian organizer, told a British newspaper that the people of Sanankoroba knew that the CFA 40,000 (about $80) they raised was a small amount in Canadian terms. But it came from their hearts, he said, and demonstrated a desire to help the friends who had helped them.

CA. 8000 B.C. Mali's present-day Saharan region is wet and fertile. Stone Age fishers and hunters live near the lakes and rivers.

CA. 4000 B.C. Rainfall begins to decrease. As the climate becomes hotter and drier, the local people learn to gather root crops and to raise livestock. Artists record pictures of their lives on rock walls.

400 B.C. The climate of the Sahara is well established as desert.

A.D. 100 Middle Eastern traders introduce the camel to northern Mali.

300 A federation of kingdoms called the Ghana Empire emerges, gaining its wealth from Saharan trade. Kumbi Saleh is its capital.

1076 The Almoravids—an Islamic Berber dynasty—send troops to destroy the Ghana Empire and take control of their trade routes.

CA. 1230 Sundiata Keita leads a successful war of independence against the Sosso kingdom, forming the rich and powerful Mali Empire.

1324 Mansa Musa, the Mali Empire's ruler, makes his famous pilgrimage to Mecca, Saudi Arabia. As a result, Islamic scholars begin to come to Mali, establishing the cities of Tombouctou and Gao as centers of learning and civilization.

CA. 1350 The Songhai Empire begins to increase in size and strength as the Mali Empire declines.

1591 Moroccan leader Ahmed al-Mansur conquers the Songhai Empire.

1600s Bambara kingdoms Ségou and Kaarta rise in prominence, becoming wealthy in part from slave trading. Colonial plantations in the Americas increasingly demand slaves to meet their labor needs.

1827 Frenchman René-Auguste Caillié leaves North Africa, disguised as an Arab, and travels across the Sahara to Tombouctou, becoming the first European to reach the city and return alive.

1852 Al-Hajj Umar, an Islamic scholar and skilled military commander, founds the Tukulor realm as the result of a jihad. The Tall dynasty begins to unite various small kingdoms.

1887 The French sign the Treaty of Bissandougou with Samory Touré, a strong Malinke leader who holds political control over much of southern Mali.

1904 France reorganizes its territory in West Africa to form the Federation of French West Africa. Under French colonial rule, Mali becomes known as French Sudan.

1923 Moussa B. Travélé publishes *Proverbes et contes Bambara* (Bambara Proverbs and Tales) in French.

1930s French-educated Malians—about 5 percent of the population—
staff part of the colonial administration in French Sudan. The rest
of the people become the object of the French policy of "assimilation,"
which seeks to make them French.

1940 France falls to Nazi Germany in World War II (1939–1945). French West
Africa comes under the control of the pro-Nazi Vichy government, but many
Malians fight with the Free French resistance.

1946 West African leaders meet in Bamako to found the continent's first interterritorial party.

1960 On September 22, the independent Republic of Mali is established. Modibo Keita
becomes its first president.

1969 Moussa Traoré becomes president of Mali after Keita is overthrown. Traoré rules as
a dictator.

1970s Drought devastates Mali, eroding traditional Tuareg society, when up to half of their
herds die from lack of food and water.

1984 Drought devastates the nation, and dissatisfaction with Traoré's military-style
government grows.

1987 Director Soulemane Cisse's film *Yeelen* (Brightness) wins awards at the important film
festival in Cannes, France. Salif Keita's solo album *Soro* becomes an international hit.

1992 Alpha O. Konare becomes Mali's first freely elected president, one year after Amadou T.
Touré leads an army coup against Traoré's regime. The country passes a new
constitution.

1996 Lighting the Flamme de la Paix (peace flame) in Tombouctou celebrates a peace agreement between rebel northerners and the government of Mali.

2002 Konare completes his second term as president, and Malians choose Amadou T. Touré as
their new president. The French president announces the cancellation of 40 percent of
Mali's debt to France. Mali hosts the African Cup of Nations soccer tournament. Gold
surpasses cotton as Mali's main export earner.

2003 Former president Konare becomes chair of the African Union (AU). Author Baba Wagué
Diakité's *The Magic Gourd* retells an old tale of animal wisdom.

2004 Drought and locusts reduce Mali's cereal harvest by as much as 45 percent,
threatening one million Malians with food shortages or starvation.

2005 Blues musician Ali Farka Touré releases *In the Heart of the Moon*. Actress
Aissa Maiga appears in the internationally successful film *Caché* (Hidden).

2006 Bamako, Mali, hosts the World Social Forum in January. Musician Ali
Farka Touré dies.

COUNTRY NAME Republic of Mali

AREA 478,842 square miles (1,240,192 sq. km)

MAIN LANDFORMS Sahara, Sahel, Niger Delta, Bandiagara Ridge, Dogon Plateau, Hombori Mountains, Manding Mountains

HIGHEST POINT Mount Hombori Tondo, 3,789 feet (1,155 m)

LOWEST POINT western border, 75 feet (23 m) above sea level

MAJOR RIVERS Bani, Niger, Senegal

ANIMALS antelope, crocodiles, elephants, giraffes, hippopatomuses, hyenas, leopards, lions, lizards, locusts, Mali firefinches, monkeys, mosquitoes, Nile perch (capitaine), termites

CAPITAL CITY Bamako

OTHER MAJOR CITIES Gao, Kayes, Mopti, Ségou, Sikasso, Tombouctou

OFFICIAL LANGUAGE French

MONETARY UNITY CFA (Communauté Financière Africaine) franc. 1 CFA franc = 100 centimes.

Fast Facts

Currency

MALI CURRENCY
The CFA franc is the shared common currency of eight countries in the West African region, including Mali. It is issued by the Central Bank of West African States.

Three vertical stripes of green, yellow, and red compose Mali's flag. The colors of the flag have meaning. Green stands for nature and agriculture. Yellow stands for gold, which brings the country wealth. And red represents the sacrifices made for independence.

Mali adopted its anthem, *For Africa and For You, Mali,* in 1962, after gaining independence from France. Seydou Badian Kouyaté (b. 1928) wrote the words, and Banzoumana Sissoko (1890–1987) wrote the music. This patriotic song states the willingness of Mali's citizens to give their lives for their country. The desire for a united Africa is also a theme in the anthem. The music of the anthem is based on a folk tune.

The English translation of the chorus is as follows:

> For Africa and for you, Mali,
> Our banner shall be liberty.
> For Africa and for you, Mali,
> Our fight shall be for unity.
> Oh, Mali of today,
> Oh, Mali of tomorrow,
> The fields are flowering with hope
> And hearts are thrilling with confidence.

For a link where you can listen to Mali's national anthem, visit www.vgsbooks.com.

SOULEMANE CISSE (b. 1940) Cisse, born in Bamako, is Mali's leading film director. He studied filmmaking for many years in the Soviet Union. On returning to Mali, he worked for the Ministry of Information. In 1987 his film *Yeelen* was the first African film ever to win awards at the international film festival in Cannes, France. It is about the origins of African society, and it highlights magic.

CHEICK MODIBO DIARRA (b. 1952) Dr. Diarra is the director of NASA's Mars Exploration Program Education project. Born in Mali, he works at Caltech (California Institute of Technology), in Pasadena, California. In 1998 the United Nations appointed him goodwill ambassador for UNESCO (United Nations Educational, Scientific, and Cultural Organization). In this role and as the founder of the Pathfinder Foundation, Diarra promotes science and technology education in Mali and elsewhere.

SALIF KEITA (b. 1942) Keita, Mali's most famous soccer player, was born in Bamako and played soccer in school. When he was fifteen, he joined a professional team, Real (Royal) Bamako. In 1970 he became the first winner of the African Player of the Year Award. The Malian Football [Soccer] Federation named Keita as president in 2005.

SALIF KEITA (b. 1949) Born in Djoliba, Keita is sometimes called the Golden Voice of Africa. He is a descendant of Sundiata Keita. Keita was born an albino (a person or animal born without pigment, usually characterized by milky skin, colorless hair, and pink or blue eyes with red pupils), resulting in social discrimination. In Bamako he joined the popular Rail Band—so named because the band played at the Bamako railway station. In 1973 he began to change traditional Malian griot music into his own highly successful variation. In 1984 Keita moved to Paris. His 1986 solo album *Soro* was the best-selling African record to that date. His music blends West African rhythms with styles from Cuba, Spain, and the Islamic world, as well as with synthesizers and electric guitars.

SUNDIATA KEITA (ca. 1210–ca.1260) Sundiata founded the Mali Empire in West Africa. Born Mari Djata, he became known as Sundiata (the Lion Prince). He transformed the Keita family's small kingdom around Kanganaa into the core of the Mali Empire. The Mali Empire's control of trade and gold made it one of the largest and richest of Africa's ancient empires. Sundiata blended Islamic and traditional African religious beliefs, and his followers believed he could do magic. When he died, the Mali Empire included most of western Mali and parts of Senegal and Guinea. Griots have depicted Sundiata as a hero-god for many centuries.

AISSA MAIGA (b. 1975) Movie actress Maiga was born in France to African parents but grew up in Mali. In 2005 she appeared in French director Michael Haneke's psychological thriller *Caché (Hidden)*, which was released to great success internationally. The story involves France's difficult historical relations with Algeria.

OUMOU SANGARÉ (b.1968) Born in Bamako, Sangaré is known as the Songbird of Wassoulou. She is the leading singer and songwriter of the Wassoulou sound. She blends the traditional melodies with mainstream styles. Her first album *Moussoulou* (Women, released in 1991) sold over 200,000 legal copies in Africa and Europe. Many more illegal copies were sold. In 1995 she toured the world. Her songs promote issues many African women feel deeply about: freedom of choice in marriage and earning respect from men.

CHRIS SEYDOU (1949–1994) Seydou was a Malian fashion designer who introduced bogolan (Malian mud cloth) to the international fashion world. He started working in tailor shops in Mali when he was sixteen. By twenty-six, he was a designer in Paris. He simplified some of the designs and used them on high-fashion European clothing, such as miniskirts. He sometimes worked with famous French designer Yves Saint Laurent.

OUSMANE SY (b. 1951) Sy is a well-known Malian democracy activist. He promotes decision making at the local level, rather than at the national level. Over time, he has worked with village elders in more than eleven thousand villages to get their support for the democratic system. His work has led to the construction of new wells, health centers, and schools in rural areas. In 2005 Belgium awarded him the International Development Prize for his contributions to democracy in the developing world.

AMADOU TOUMANI TOURÉ (b. 1948) Born in Mopti, Touré as a young man studied to be a teacher. But in 1969, he entered the military instead. In 1991, after days of violent riots demanding democracy, Touré led the army in overthrowing President Traoré and his military rule. Touré supervised Mali's transition to a democratically elected government in 1992. His actions won him respect. In 2002 Touré became Mali's president in a peaceful, democratic election.

AMINATA DRAMANE TRAORÉ (b. 1942) Traoré is an author and politician, with a Ph.D. in psychology. She opposes the economic policies of developed countries toward developing countries like Mali. She points out the policies favor the already wealthy countries. From 1997 to 2000, she served as the minster of Culture and Tourism of Mali. She is the associate coordinator of the International Network for Cultural Diversity. She is involved in the World Social Forum, which met in Mali in 2006.

BAMAKO Bamako, the capital city, is home to many of Mali's ethnic groups. Located on the Niger, Bamako is shady, relaxed, and welcoming. It is one of the most traditional African capitals, meaning it is also dusty and crowded. The bustling markets offer arts and crafts as well as everyday items. The National Museum's exhibits feature Mali's history and contemporary life. Muso Kunda (from the woman's side) is a museum dedicated to the women of Mali, with an excellent restaurant serving African food. Mali musicians play in the city's nightclubs.

DJENNÉ The Djenné Mosque, a World Heritage Site, dominates Djenné's central square. This impressive mud-brick mosque dates from 1907 but sits on the site where mosques have stood since the thirteenth century. Every Monday, Mali's most colorful market is held in front of the mosque.

DOGON COUNTRY Located in the Mopti region, Dogon Country is Mali's most popular tourist destination. Hikers trekking through the region see spectacular cliffs, breathtaking views, and vast plains. Dogon villages are built into the sides of the cliffs, and traditional dances are performed for tourists.

GAO This desert town on the Niger River was the capital of the powerful Songhai Empire. The hospitable Tuareg and Songhai population of Gao are known for their cooking. Visitors can take river excursions to *la dune rose* (the pink dune), a tall sand dune outside town where people used to meet to practice magic. The view from the top is worth the climb.

KAYES Kayes was the capital of French Sudan during the colonial era. Located on the Senegal River, Kayes still has many European-style buildings and boulevards. It is also one of the hottest towns in Africa. From Kayes you can visit Baoulé Bend National Park.

KIDAL Saharan Kidal, near the Adrar des Iforas chain of beautiful mountains, is home to the majority of Mali's Tuareg. Livestock herding and production of handicrafts are the livelihoods of the residents. Nearby are ancient rock art sites and other picturesque villages.

MOPTI Mopti is sometimes called the Venice of Mali because, like the Italian city, it is built on islands. It is one of the busiest ports on the Niger River, selling and trading everything from fish and salt to mud cloth and patterned wool blankets.

TOMBOUCTOU The ancient city of Tombouctou is a World Heritage Site, although there is not a lot left to see. In one day, visitors can easily view the city's mosques, houses of famous explorers, the ancient university, and other sites. Tour guides offer camel rides into the Sahara and to visit Tuareg camps outside the city.

cash crop: a crop, such as cotton, grown to be sold for money rather than used to feed a family

colony: a territory ruled and occupied by a foreign power

desert: an area that receives less than 10 inches (25cm) of rain a year

desertification: the process of land turning into desert, caused by a combination of human and climate factors: drought, clearing land of plant life, and overuse of dry lands

griot: an oral historian of West Africa, called *djeliw* in Mali. Griots keep history alive with praise songs recording the deeds of rulers and heroes through the ages.

gross domestic product (GDP): the value of goods and services produced in a country in a year. Gross national product (GNP) also counts foreign income.

Islam: a worldwide religion founded by the prophet Muhammad. Followers are called Muslims. The holy book of Islam, the Quran, contains Muhammad's messages from Allah (God).

literacy: the ability to read and write a basic sentence. A country's literacy is one of the indicators of its level of human development.

mansa: the title of the king or ruler in ancient Mali

mosque: an Islamic place of worship and prayer

mud cloth: cotton cloth dyed with designs painted in dark mud by the Bambara people of Mali

nationalist: a person who wants independence and feels supreme loyalty toward a nation

nomad: a herder who moves with animals in search of pasture and water

oasis: a fertile place in the desert where underground water comes to the surface

patriarchal society: a social system in which men have more political, economic, and social power than women

Quran: the holy book of Islam. The prophet Muhammad dictated the book starting in A.D. 610. Muslims believe these scriptures come from God.

Africa South of the Sahara 2005. London: Europa Publications, 2005.
The long section on Mali in this annual publication covers the country's recent history, geography, and culture, as well as provides a detailed look at the economy, politics, and government of the country. Statistics and sources are also included.

"Background Note: Mali." *U.S. Department of State, Bureau of African Affairs*. 2005.
http://www.state.gov/r/pa/ei/bgn/2828.htm (October 2005).
The background notes of the U.S. State Department supplies a profile of Mali's people, history, government, political conditions, economy, and more.

BBC News. 2006.
http://www.bbc.co.uk (January 2006).
The World Edition of the BBC (British Broadcasting Corporation) News is updated throughout the day, every day. The BBC is a source for comprehensive news coverage about Mali and also provides a country profile.

Brook, Larry. *Daily Life in Ancient and Modern Timbuktu*. Minneapolis: Lerner Publications Company, 1999.
A title in the Cities through Time series, this lushly illustrated book presents the history of the city of Tombouctou. The author follows the city from its beginning as a camping site for Tuareg nomads, through its height as a center of trade and learning in the 1500s, and on to its modern-day state of decline.

Central Intelligence Agency (CIA). "Mali." *The World Factbook*. 2006.
http://www.cia.gov/cia/publications/factbook/geos/ml.html (January 2006).
This CIA website provides facts and figures on Mali's geography, people, government, economy, communications, transportation, military, and more.

Curtin, Philip D., ed. *Africa Remembered: Narratives by West Africans from the Era of the Slave Trade*. Prospect Heights, IL: Waveland, 1997.
A collection of ten rare, personal recollections of Africans tells the story of the West African slave trade from an African point of view. The book includes the autobiographical tale Abu Bakr al-Siddiq of Tombouctou.

Cutter, Charles H. *Africa 2004*. Harpers Ferry, WV: Stryker-Post, 2004.
The article on Mali in this annual volume of the World Today series provides a moderately detailed look at the recent culture, politics, and economics of the country.

The Diagram Group. *History of West Africa*. New York: Facts on File, 2003.
Part of the History of Africa series, this title presents a historical overview of the region that includes Mali. Details of ancient kingdoms, colonialism, independence movements, and modern times are well illustrated with drawings, maps, and charts.

Diakité, Baba Wagué. *The Magic Gourd.* **New York: Scholastic, 2003.**
This retelling of a traditional Malian tale about Brother Rabbit (Dogo Zan) is also beautifully illustrated by the author. Notes in the back explain the Bambara words, mud cloth patterns, and the role of praise songs.

The Economist. **2005.**
http://www.economist.com (January 2006).
A weekly British magazine available online or in print, the *Economist* provides in-depth coverage of international news, including Mali's political and economic news. The *Economist* also offers country profiles with relevant articles as well as some statistics at www.economist.com/countries.

Imperato, Pascal James. *Historical Dictionary of Mali.* **3rd ed. Lanham, MD: Scarecrow Press, 1996.**
A very useful reference book, this dictionary includes short articles on culture, economics, history, politics, and social issues, as well as informative entries on people, places, and events. Maps, a timeline, and a bibliography are included.

Jenkins, Mark. *To Timbuktu.* **New York: William Morrow, 1997.**
This is the record of the author's journey down the Niger River. Jenkins writes about being attacked by bees, hippos, and crocodiles. Eventually leaving the river, he buys a motorcycle to drive across the desert to Tombouctou. Jenkins also tells the fascinating and gruesome tales of European adventurers who tried to reach the city in the 1800s.

"Mali." *University of Pennsylvania, African Studies Center.* **n.d.**
http://www.sas.upenn.edu/African_Studies/Country_Specific/Mali.html. (January 2006).
The African Studies Center offers many links to resources to find information about Mali. The mission statement of the center says it is a "center where researchers, students and cultural and business entities come to gain knowledge of contemporary and historical Africa."

Population Reference Bureau. **2005.**
http://www.prb.org (October 2005).
PRB's annual statistics provide in-depth demographics on Mali's population, including birthrates and death rates, infant mortality rates, and other statistics relating to health, environment, education, employment, family planning, and more. Special articles cover environmental and health issues.

USAID in Africa: Mali. **2006.**
http://www.usaid.gov/locations/sub-saharan_africa/countries/mali/
This site records the work of USAID (U.S. Agency for International Development), an independent federal government agency, in Mali. Spending less than one-half of 1 percent of the U.S. federal budget, USAID works around the world to promote fair economic growth, to open societies to businesses, to expand political freedom, to improve health and education, and to empower women. USAID goals include preventing conflict, reducing HIV/AIDS, aiding agriculture, and encouraging good management of natural resources. Photos of Mali are on display at USAID's photo gallery: http://www.dec.org/partners/afr/photogallery/search_results.cfm.

The African Music Encyclopedia
http://africanmusic.org/home.html

In the 1990s, Malian music strongly influenced the international "World Beat" movement. It remains popular in Mali and around the world. Read about Mali's vibrant music scene on this site.

"Bambara: The Art of Existence in Mali." *Museum for African Art.*
http://www.africanart.org/html/exhibitions.html

A description of an exhibit in New York City, in 2002, featuring Malian art objects, photographs, and more, is found on this site.

Benanav, Michael. *Men of Salt: Crossing the Sahara on the Caravan of White Gold.* Guilford, CT: The Lyons Press, 2006.

This book is Benanav's account of joining a caravan of salt miners as they make their perilous journey across the Sahara.

Bond, George, ed. *The Heritage Library of African People: West Africa.* New York: Rosen Publishing, 1996.

This series of books for younger readers describes the environment, lifestyles, customs, languages, and more of the African continent's peoples. Titles about Mali's ethnic groups are *Dogon* by Chukwuma Azuonye; *Songhay*, by Tunde Adeleke; and *Malinke* and *Soninke*, both by C. O. Nwanunobi.

Diakité, Baba Wagué. *The Hatseller and the Monkeys.* New York: Scholastic, 1999.

A retelling of a Malian folktale about a group of monkeys who steal a hat-seller's hats. The author, who grew up in a small village in Mali, illustrated this book with paintings on ceramic tile.

Festival in the Desert. CD. Murs Erigné, France: Triban Union, 2003.

This exciting music CD was recorded live at the 2003 Festival in the Desert in Essakane, near Tombouctou, Mali. Northern and southern Malian musicians, including stars Ali Farka Touré and Oumou Sangaré, were joined by musicians from Mauritania, Niger, Europe, and the United States.

Finley, Carol. *The Art of African Masks.* Minneapolis: Lerner Publications Company, 1999.

The author explains how African masks are made and what their functions are in society. Some of Mali's mask-making ethnic groups are included in this book. Color photos show masks and mask dancers in action.

Jelloun, Tahar Ben. *Islam Explained.* Toronto: University of Toronto Press, 2004.

This book for anyone who wants to learn about Islam offers a clear introduction to the history and main beliefs of the religion. Presented in question-and-answer format between the author and young questioners, the book also defines words often heard in the news, such as *terrorist*, *crusade*, *jihad*, and *fundamentalist*.

Lange, Karen E. "Djénné, West Africa's Eternal City." *National Geographic*, June 2001, 100–117.

Wonderful photos enliven this article about the people and the Great Mosque of Djénné. More photos and notes can be found at www.nationalgeographic.com/ngm/0106.

Life on Earth (La vie sur terre). **Directed by Abderrahman Sissako. Produced by Haut et Court, La Sept-Arte. DVD. New York: Fox Lorber Studio, 2000.**

Filmed in Sokolo, Mali, this movie follows a man returning from Paris to his village in Mali for the beginning of the year 2000. But he sees that nothing has changed for Mali with the new millennium.

Mali Embassy
http://www.maliembassy.us/new_site/default.htm

The embassy of Mali's official site offers information on travel, tourism, government information, the national anthem, the economy, and articles on Mali.

Montgomery, Bertha Vining, and Constance Nabwire. *Cooking the West African Way*. **Minneapolis: Lerner Publications Company, 2002.**

Part of the Easy Menu Ethnic Cookbooks series, this book offers cultural information as well as recipes from the countries around southern Mali. The people of these countries share many foods and lifestyle patterns with Mali's ethnic groups.

"Mali." Oxfam's *Cool Planet*.
http://www.oxfam.org.uk/coolplanet/ontheline/explore/journey/mali/malindex.htm

This is the website of On the Line, a project in the year 2000. It explores the lives of people in the eight countries lying along the zero-degree meridian line: Mali, Togo, Ghana, Burkina Faso, Algeria, Spain, France, and the United Kingdom. The project used media, music, arts, and formal education to look at the countries.

Peace Corps Kids Explore the World: Mali
http://www.peacecorps.gov/kids/world/africa/mali.html

This site has firsthand accounts of everyday life in Mali. Learn about Peace Corps work in Mali in the areas of agriculture, business development, the environment, and health.

vgsbooks.com
http://www.vgsbooks.com

Visit vgsbooks.com, the home page of the Visual Geography Series ®, which is updated regularly. You can get linked to all sorts of useful online information, including geographical, historical, demographic, cultural, and economic websites. The vgsbooks.com site is a great resource for late-breaking news and statistics.

Welch, Galbraith. *The Unveiling of Timbuctoo*. **Reprint. New York: W. Morrow, year. New York: Carroll & Graf, 1991.**

This is the story of Frenchman René-Auguste Caillié, the first European to reach Tombouctou and return alive. For many years, his amazing trip was dismissed as fake. In 1934 Galbraith Welch retraced Caillié's path across the Sahara and tells of her own adventures doing so.

Winter, Jeanette. *My Baby*. **New York: Farrar, Straus and Giroux, 2001.**

This picture book demonstrates the centuries-old Malian technique of making mud-dyed cloth. It also captures the sights and sounds of a Malian village.

69; natural resources, 16–17; neighbors of, 8; patriarchal social system, 23, 43; Republic of Mali, 33, 67, 68; Third Republic of Mali, 37; topography of, 8–10, 12; Trans-Sahara Plan, 36

Malian people, 38–39; ethnic and language groups, 39–42

maps: physical, 11; political, 6

Mauritania, 8, 13, 23–24, 25, 31, 35

Niger, 25, 31, 52, 64

Nigeria, 12, 26

North Africa, 5, 9, 24, 28, 46, 66

parasites, 45, 46

political parties, 32–33; Alliance for Democracy in Mali (ADEMA), 35; Democratic Union of the Malian People (UDPM), 35; Popular Militia, 34; Rassemblement Démocratique Africain (RDA), 32; Union Soudanaise (US), 33

ports, 19, 20

Quran, 47, 48, 52. *See also* religion: Islam

Ramadan, 49, 56. *See also* religion: Islam

recipe, 57

regimes: Keita regime, 33–34, 67; Traoré regime, 34–35, 67

regions and landforms: Adrar des Iforas, 9, 72; Bandiagara Ridge, 10, 68; Dogon Country, 41–42, 63, 64, 72; Dogon Plateau, 10, 68; Hombori Mountains, 10, 12, 68; Manding Mountains, 12, 68; Mount Hombori Tondo, 12, 68; Niger Delta, 10, 68; Sahara, 23, 24, 25, 27, 28, 33, 36, 41, 66, 68, 72; Sahel, 8–10, 13, 14, 34, 40, 68

religion, 48–50; Allah (God), 48–49, 56; Christianity, 28, 29, 50; hajj, 24; Islam, 5, 7, 18, 19, 20–21, 24, 25, 26–28, 29, 30, 36, 43, 46–47, 48–50, 52, 57, 70; Islamic brotherhoods, 49; Mecca, 25, 49, 56, 66; Muhammad, 48–49, 56; syncretism, 50

rivers, 12–13: Bani, 10, 12, 15, 19, 68; Congo, 12; Niger, 4, 5–6, 10, 12, 15, 16, 17, 18, 19, 20, 22, 25, 28, 30, 40, 61, 63, 64, 68, 72; Nile, 12, 15, 57; Senegal, 12, 19, 40, 64, 68, 72

Sahara. *See* regions and landforms

Sahel. *See* regions and landforms

salt trade, 24, 63

Saudi Arabia, 25, 48–49, 66

Ségou, 18–19, 68. *See also* kingdoms

Senegal, 8, 13, 19, 25, 27, 30–31, 32, 70

slave trade, 26–28

sports, recreation, and holidays, 55–56

Tall, Amadou. *See* dynasties: Tall

Tombouctou, 12, 20, 25, 26, 28, 29, 35, 46, 52, 56, 66, 67, 68, 72

Touré, Amadou Toumani, 7, 35–36, 65, 67, 71

Traoré, Moussa. *See* regimes

United Nations (UN), 7, 36, 58–60, 70

West Africa, 7, 8, 14, 20–21, 26–27, 28, 29, 30–31, 38, 52, 54, 62, 64, 66, 67, 70

women, 47, 52, 53, 54, 67, 71, 72; female genital mutilation (FGM), 44; roles of, 43–44

World War II, 31–32, 67

Captions for photos appearing on cover and chapter openers:

Cover: Djenné is an island town in the Bani River. It is one of the oldest towns in West Africa. Like Tombouctou, Djenné profited from trans-Saharan trade in the 1300s and 1400s. But unlike Tombouctou, Djenné continued to prosper even as Tombouctou declined.

pp. 4–5 The sun sets over the Niger River in Mali. The Niger River takes its name from the word *gber-n-igheren*, which means "river of rivers" in the North African Berber language.

pp. 8–9 The Sahel region of Mali is a transitional zone between the arid Sahara and the fertile Niger River delta.

pp. 22–23 Ancient paintings reveal part of Mali's early history. Thousands of years ago, artists worked on the rock walls of caves and overhangs. They depicted large animals—such as giraffes, elephants, and rhinoceroses—that inhabited the Sahara's grasslands and forests. Water animals—crocodiles, hippopotamuses, and fish, for example—also appear in the cave illustrations. Scholars study this artistic evidence and other archaeological clues to learn about the history of Mali's climate and lifestyles.

pp. 38–39 Members of a women's finance group in Bamako share a laugh.

pp. 48–49 Dogon dancers wearing masks perform at a dama celebration. The dama celebration takes place every thirteen years to honor the spirits of Dogon ancestors.

pp. 58–59 Tourists follow a Tuareg camel train on its way to Tombouctou.

Photo Acknowledgments
The images in this book are used with the permission of: © Warren Jacobs/Art Directors, pp. 4-5; © XNR Productions, pp. 6, 11; © Peter Langer-Associated Media Group, pp. 8-9, 48-49; © Eugene Schulz, pp. 10, 43, 44 (left); © TRIP/Art Directors, pp. 12, 47; PhotoDisc Royalty-Free by Getty Images, p. 14; © Royalty-Free/CORBIS, p. 15; © Remi Benali/CORBIS, p. 16; © Mary Jelliffe/Art Directors, pp. 17, 18-19, 40, 41, 44 (right), 58-59, 63, 64; © age fotostock/SuperStock, pp. 20-21; © Jane Sweeney/Art Directors, pp. 22-23; © MPI/Hulton Archive/Getty Images, p. 27; © Hulton Archive/Getty Images, p. 29; © AFP/Getty Images, p. 33; © Charles & Josette Lenars/CORBIS, p. 34; © John Thys/AFP/Getty Images, p. 36; © Crispin Hughes/Panos Pictures, pp. 38-39; © Jamie Carstairs/Art Directors, pp. 42, 55; Centers for Disease and Control and Prevention Public Health Image Library/James Gathany, p. 45; © Giacomo Pirozzi/Panos Pictures, p. 46; © Dean Fox/SuperStock, p. 51 (left); © Sean Sprague/Photo Agora, p. 51 (right); AP/Wide World Photos, p. 54 (top); © Hector Mata/AFP/Getty Images, p. 54 (bottom); © Issouf Sanogo/AFP/Getty Images, p. 56; © Jason Laure, p. 61; Audrius Tomonis—www.banknotes.com, p. 68; © Laura Westlund/Independent Picture Service, p. 69.

Front Cover: © Remi Benali/CORBIS. Back Cover: NASA.